Lı

Rea

K A

Pippin Publishing

Copyright © 1993 by Pippin Publishing Corporation
85 Ellesmere Road
Suite 232
Scarborough, Ontario
M1R 4B9

Edited by Dyanne Rivers
Designed by John Zehethofer
Printed and bound in Canada by Friesens

Canadian Cataloguing in Publication Data

Feathers, Karen M. 1941-
    Infotext: reading and learning

(The Pippin teacher's library ; 10)
Includes bibliographical references.
ISBN 0-88751-056-6

1. Reading comprehension. 2. Content area reading. 3. Reading(Elementary). 4. Reading (Secondary). 5. Reading (Higher education). I. Title. II.
Series.

LB1050.45.F42 1992   428.4′3   C92-095080-9

ISBN 0-88751-056-6

10   9   8   7   6   5   4

CONTENTS

To my parents whose love and support has made all things possible—"For now I know who I am and what I am, and that is simply me."

. . . .

PREFACE

Infotexts are the books, textbooks, journals, newspapers and computer manuals that we read to gather information about particular topics. They may be oral—lectures and speeches—as well as written. The size, shape, appearance and content of infotexts may change from year to year, but they remain the same in one important way—they deal with information.

For more years than I care to remember, I've worked with students of varying ages to help them become better readers. My first position was as a remedial reading teacher for grades seven to twelve. Even then, when I knew much less than I do now about the reading process, I was aware that students had much more difficulty reading content texts than fictional narratives, and I began to spend more and more time helping them overcome this difficulty.

Over the years, my interest in informational reading has continued and grown. I've read many books on the subject, but have found none that reflect my beliefs. Though these books are packed with information about readability formulas, student motivation and activities designed to increase students' learning, they focus on what *teachers* can do—the activities are, for the most part, generated and controlled by the teacher.

In this book, I am presenting an alternative because I believe that the best way to help readers is to provide them with opportunities to help themselves. While teachers may initiate some of the activities suggested, the activities themselves are controlled by the students. Rather than following a study guide developed by a teacher to reflect the teacher's ideas, students develop their own notes, reflecting their own ideas about what is important and how the text is organized.

If we want people to swim, we must be prepared to help them into the lake — they can't learn by sitting on the dock and dangling their feet in the water. I throw students into the lake of content reading, but not by themselves. I throw everyone in together — and I jump in with them. If someone starts to sink, we can all help push him or her to the surface. While I provide support, I don't do the swimming for them.

If students are to learn how to read infotexts, they must read real texts, not bits and pieces of texts. And teachers cannot do the reading and thinking for them. Supporting their attempts does not mean providing them with study guides, but rather with opportunities to explore and talk about their discoveries.

This book is about reading and learning. We read infotexts in order to learn. Reading affords us the opportunity to learn not only *through* reading but also *about* reading. When we do things in our classrooms that help students become better readers, they will also learn, through the reading they do, about the topics they are studying.

Infotext: Reading and Learning reflects my belief that reading and learning are not separate activities. Rather, they happen simultaneously every time we open a book. I invite you to continue in this book to read, to learn to read, and to learn.

. . . .

WHY TEACH

CONTENT READING?

Whenever teachers gather to talk shop, they're likely to make comments like these:

- "I teach ninth grade social studies. Students should know how to read before they get to my class."
- "I teach science. What do I know about teaching reading?"
- "I have to cover what's in my math book. I can't take time to teach reading."
- "I teach reading during reading time and science during science time."
- "I can't teach reading all the time."

These are the most common reasons teachers cite for not teaching reading to students during content classes such as math, science, history, art, music, accounting, psychology and physical education. I've heard them over and over as I work with teachers to integrate reading instruction into content classes.

I include them because they raise important issues. While teachers are expected to "cover" certain content material in their classes, many content teachers have had little or no instruction in teaching reading. In addition, because reading is taught as a separate subject, we have come to believe that it *should* be taught separately. The concentration on reading instruction in the early grades also suggests that reading is a skill learned in elementary school, preferably in the first three or four grades, then applied as learning continues. In other words, the organization of our schools and our own training as teachers foster these beliefs.

While these beliefs continue to be pervasive, they don't reflect current understandings of reading instruction or learning in general. We now know that reading is best taught when integrated into all subject areas, that learning how to read never stops, and that reading instruction need not take time from the learning of content.

What would it take to interest you in teaching reading in the content areas? What if I could show you strategies — things to do with students in your own classroom — that do not decrease the time spent on content while increasing the amount of learning? And what if these strategies don't require you to take reading courses to gain an in-depth understanding of reading theory? What if they are so understandable that they've been taught to parents with no background in education? Would you be interested?

I hope so, because that's what this book is about — strategies that will help students read infotexts of all descriptions with greater understanding and better retention of information. The strategies will not reduce the time spent teaching content; content is always the focus when using them.

Before we begin to discuss these strategies, however, we need to consider two important questions: why teach content reading and why teach reading during content classes?

Why Teach Content Reading?

We never stop learning to read.

First we learn to read, then we read to learn. This statement represents the thinking that has, for years, dominated not only reading instruction, but also instruction in the content areas. It implies that students are first taught a skill called "reading," so that they can then use this skill to learn by reading a variety of informational material such as content textbooks.

The dichotomy between "learning to read" and "reading" suggests two things: first, that at some point we stop learning to read and begin reading to learn; and, second, that if we have successfully learned how to read — if we are labeled proficient readers — we should be able to read anything.

My own experiences tell me that neither of these suppositions is true. I have certainly had trouble reading many texts since I achieved what anyone would identify as reading "proficiency." For instance, when my son, Jeff, started reading science-fiction stories in his teens, I began reading them too, so that we could continue to talk about books. At first, I had difficulty with the stories because they were so different from the narratives I was used to. Since then, I have become an avid science-fiction reader and no longer have difficulty with those texts.

Surely, this suggests that I have continued to learn to read. I could recount similar experiences with the mystery books I began to read only after getting hooked on mysteries on television, the statistics texts I encountered while doing graduate work, and such common reading material as income tax forms, directions for working my VCR, manuals for operating my computer, and the lease for the house I am renting. My initial encounters with all these materials — and many others — were problematic, some to the point where I wondered if I knew how to read at all. Nevertheless, in all cases, I eventually came to understand the material.

My experience, then, indicates that we are continually engaged in learning about reading. We never reach a point where we can say we have nothing more to learn. Each new text offers — indeed, demands — new learning about reading. At the same time, no one ever simply reads to learn. We are always learning about reading, even when information-gathering is uppermost in our minds. For this reason, we can never restrict learning to read to certain grade levels or to certain courses. Reading instruction is something that all teachers must do all the time. It is important to teach reading in all subject areas, so that students become not only better readers but also successful learners.

Students don't — or can't — read their textbooks.

Fred Smith, who taught social studies methods at Indiana University, and I conducted a year-long investigation of reading in junior high and high school social studies classrooms to find out what kinds of help teachers provided students in reading infotexts. We observed in four classrooms three times a week for ten weeks in the fall and, in the spring, every day for five to six weeks. We also interviewed the students and their teachers.

Disturbingly, the interviews revealed that 75 per cent of the students read no part of the textbook even though reading was assigned regularly. While we certainly didn't expect all students to read the texts, we were certainly surprised to find that such a large number did no textbook reading at all. In fact, only 5 per cent of the students usually read the text, while the remainder read varying portions.

One student who said he read part of the text was asked what — and when — he read. He replied, "I read the headings and the stuff under the pictures on the way from first period to second." Although this sounds like a minimal amount of reading, it was representative of what and how much many students read. The interviews and our observations throughout the year revealed that students went to great lengths to avoid reading the textbook, regardless of the assignments developed by teachers to ensure that they were read.

One reason students don't read their textbooks is because there is no reason to do so. In the classrooms where we observed, teachers lectured on the material covered in the readings, thereby providing all the information students needed to know. This happened even when infotext reading was assigned and even when students were expected to answer questions on the reading.

When questioned, teachers said they lectured on the material either because students didn't read the text or the text was too difficult and they believed they needed to explain it.

These explanations make sense if the focus is on learning the information in the text; however, we must recognize that, as long as the teacher provides the information, students will have no real reason to read the text to gather information for themselves. And, because they know the teacher will explain everything, there is also no reason for them to make a studious attempt to comprehend the text.

During the interviews, students also revealed that they had difficulty reading their textbooks. This was confirmed by our observations. While we were observing, we were often approached to help students find answers in the textbooks for worksheet questions. This happened as often in advanced classes as it did in "low track" classes.

There are several possible explanations for students' difficulties with textbooks:

— They have not had experiences with content texts and don't know how to read them. In the early elementary grades, most of the books used to teach reading are fictional narratives and most students learn to read these successfully. Students are exposed to far fewer informational texts and are therefore less familiar with the text structures, vocabulary, sentence structures and organizational patterns of infotexts.

— Reading strategies that students have developed and used to comprehend fictional narratives successfully do not necessarily help them understand infotexts. When they read content texts, they may not possess the necessary processing strategies or they may not know how or when to use them. If they continually fail to understand what they're reading, they will eventually give up their attempts to comprehend the text and stop opening the book.

— Students' proficiency in reading fiction suggests to them that they are capable readers. They assume that if they can read one text, they can read them all. Then, when they encounter difficulty with unfamiliar infotexts, they blame themselves for their failure to understand. They question their original assessment of their ability and decide that they aren't capable readers after all. At this point, they stop trying to deal with content texts, rationalizing continued attempts to do so as futile.

There are many problems with the textbooks.

Many textbooks are poorly written. A group of teachers reviewed a chapter on the American Civil War in a fifth-grade social studies text and came up with the following list of problems:

— Poor organization.
— Sequence of events not in order.
— Abrupt shifts in topic.
— Headings, subheadings not related.
— Subheadings not related to material contained in the section.

- Too much material covered in one chapter.
- Too many unrelated details.
- Little depth on any topic.
- Information biased.
- Vocabulary not explained.
- Vocabulary poorly explained.
- Few examples that helped students understand terms.
- Pictures not explained.
- Pictures and maps not related to information on the page.
- Poor sentence structure.
- Short, choppy sentences.
- Questions at end of chapter focus on details.
- Some questions not answerable based on information given.

One of the major problems with this chapter was the amount of information it covered. Events that led to the war, the events of the war itself, and reconstruction after the war were all covered in fourteen pages.

Another major problem was the organization of the chapter. For example, one section titled "Problems that led to the War" contained these subheadings: "Problems with Slavery," "Problems with Tariffs," and "Three Black Leaders." While the first two subheadings follow logically from the major heading, the last does not. It isn't surprising, then, that students trying to use these headings to organize information will encounter problems.

Similar problems exist in other textbooks. In an article in *American Educator*, Harriet Bernstein suggested that what she called "mentioning" is a major factor leading to many of the other problems. Responding to pressure from a variety of special-interest groups, textbook publishers attempt to cover a lot of ground in a single text. To do so, they resort to mentioning many issues, providing virtually no in-depth discussion of any of them.

This trend also contributes to organizational shortcomings, shifts in topic, a failure to explain vocabulary, and many other problems.

When students have little experience with infotexts, reading even well-written content texts can be difficult. Their problems are compounded dramatically when the infotexts they encounter are poorly written. Unfortunately, because teachers rarely acknowledge the shortcomings of these texts, students blame themselves, rather than the texts, for their difficulties. Helping students become aware of problems in the texts themselves can significantly change their attitude towards reading and increase the amount of informational reading they do.

Even well-written informational texts are structured differently from the fictional narratives students are more familiar with. Fictional narratives tend to focus on people involved in familiar actions and events that follow a basic time sequence. Infotexts often focus on unfamiliar topics that are defined, explained and described in terms of and related to other discrete items of information that are irrelevant to students' lives outside the classroom.

We're all familiar with the phenomenon of students memorizing material for tests, then promptly forgetting just about everything. Many of us have done exactly the same thing ourselves. If we want real learning to occur, the information students encounter must be relevant to them in some way. This doesn't mean that they should read only about things like bicycles, sports, skateboards or whatever else is currently of interest. It does mean that textbooks should present information in a way that it is relevant to the students for whom it is intended. This is not typically the case with content texts.

Why Teach Reading in Content Classes?

It is the best way to learn how to read infotexts.

The best way to learn anything is, of course, to do it. For example, the best way to learn how to cook is to cook, perhaps in the company of an experienced chef. Similarly, the best way to learn how to read a content text is to do so with support from someone experienced in reading this type of material — that is, a content teacher.

It results in better learning of content material.

Teaching reading in content classrooms does much more than help students learn to read their texts. The techniques developed and used to improve reading proficiency also help deepen students' understanding and, therefore, learning of the material. Many teachers are reluctant to teach what they consider to be "reading skills" during content classes because they fear it will reduce the amount of time available to learn the content. In fact, engaging students in sound comprehension activities contributes to increased learning of content material in less time.

It helps students become independent learners.

When students are able to understand their content texts without assistance, teachers no longer need to spend time telling them what the text said. This frees class time for activities that provide deeper understanding, expand on text information, provoke critical evaluation of information, and present students with opportunities to apply what they've learned. These activities help students develop the interests and skills to ensure that they become lifelong learners capable of self-motivated learning.

Summary

All reading involves learning, not only of content, but also about the reading process itself. For a variety of reasons, many students have difficulty reading infotexts and need help to deal with these texts if learning is to occur.

Instruction that involves sound comprehension activities results not only in more proficient reading but also in more effective learning of content. Content reading must be taught, but how does one begin?

This book will begin by taking a brief look at the theoretical basis for reading and content instruction. Then, various classroom strategies that can be used to enable students to become independent readers and learners will be explained. These strategies differ from instructional methods that focus on things *teachers* can do so that students learn the material covered. They focus on things *students* can do to read and learn more effectively. In fact, if the strategies are successful, they will become obsolete — students will internalize and use them whenever they read informational material. Each strategy is designed to focus on content. This ensures that we are never simply teaching reading but, rather, are introducing activities that help students learn *how* to read while, at the same time, increasing their knowledge of the subject. Jerome Harste says that any instance of reading affords the opportunity to "learn reading, to learn about reading, and to learn through reading." The strategies described in this book provide the opportunities for all this learning to occur.

THE BASIS

OF CONTENT READING

While we don't need to immerse ourselves in reading courses to teach content reading, we do need to understand some basics if we are to make wise decisions about the instructional strategies we use with students. Is all reading the same? What factors affect reading? How do we read? What do proficient readers do? What do we know about learning that can help us?

Is All Reading the Same?

A belief that reading is a generic skill has predominated for many years. We see it in materials used for reading instruction in schools and in radio and television commercials for programs that purport to teach reading—"There are only forty-seven sounds in the English language. Learn these sounds and you can read anything."

A generic skill is one that, once learned, can be applied in any situation. For example, if I learn the generic skill of hammering a nail, it follows that I can then hammer any nail. If I learn how to ride a bicycle, I can then ride any bicycle. The same reasoning applied to reading says that, once I learn how to read, I can then read anything. This view assumes that if students can read words, they can read sentences; if they can read sentences, they can read stories; and, if they can read stories, they then have what it takes to read social studies texts, science texts, and other informational materials.

We now know, however, that reading is not a generic skill. Even adults who are able to read novels, poetry and informational material proficiently often have trouble with insurance policies, tax forms, directions for putting together swing sets, computer manuals, and informational material on unfamiliar topics.

Actually, there are no truly generic skills. Just because I can ride a standard bicycle doesn't mean that I can ride a ten-speed racing bike. Similarly, different nails are used in different materials for different purposes, and they are not all hammered the same way. We learn things not in isolation, but in a context. We learn how to hammer a particular kind of nail into a particular material using a particular hammer.

If the situation changes — if the nails, material or hammer are different — then what I have already learned may actually be a hindrance. Consider someone who has learned to hit a large, long nail very hard to drive it deep into wooden beams. Now he has a short, slim nail that he wants to drive into a plaster wall to hang a picture. If he applies his learned nail-driving skill in this situation, he may crack the plaster, bend the nail, hit his thumb, or, even if all else goes well, drive the nail too far into the wall.

Nothing we learn can be transferred directly to all situations. However, we do use what we already know to deal with new situations. When we must hammer a new kind of nail, we use what we already know from past experiences with nails, plaster and picture-hanging and put it all together to hypothesize what to do. We draw on all our relevant past experiences to deal with new situations. If the new experience is very similar to our past experiences, our behavior may be very similar to past behavior. But if the new experience is dissimilar, our previous experiences may not be helpful at all.

What does this mean for reading? Like everything else, reading is learned in a context. We learn how to read particular texts and, depending on the text encountered and the instruction we receive, develop strategies for achieving understanding.

When the context changes — when we are faced with different material to read or different purposes for reading — we use what we have learned from previous reading experiences. However, what was learned during previous experiences may not work in the new situation. Strategies developed for hitting one kind of nail don't work with all nails, and strategies learned for reading one kind of text don't necessarily work with all texts.

What Factors Affect Reading?

Reading always takes place within a context and is specific to the context that surrounds the act of reading. Three factors — the text, the reader and the context of the reading situation — influence reading. While each will be discussed separately, they are not, in fact, entirely separate. Rather, they overlap and interact to affect the reading process.

THE TEXT

The vocabulary, sentence structure and organizational patterns of reading materials vary. While fictional narratives differ from poems and infotexts, there are also differences within the types. Just as all stories are not alike, not all infotexts are the same. A history text and a science text are as different as a history text and a story. Because each needs to be read differently, these variations affect the reading process.

Additionally, the readability of texts also varies. Some texts are well-written and offer support for the reader. They use familiar sentence structures, are well-organized, provide links between ideas, and define terminology clearly. Other texts are not as well-written and may be disorganized, contain sentences that are too simple or too complex, and fail to define terminology or link major concepts. Texts such as these are not "reader-friendly," making comprehension difficult.

THE READER

The reader also affects the reading process. A reader's physical and emotional state affects how she approaches reading experiences. Is she tired? Hungry? Happy? Upset? Any one of these can — and will — make a difference in how readers approach texts.

The reader doesn't operate in isolation but interacts with the reading material and the situation in which the reading occurs. A student whose parents are divorcing might be upset and unable to concentrate on reading a science text. On the other hand, the same student may eagerly read a story about a child of divorced parents or informational material about coping with divorce.

The prior knowledge of the reader is also important. A reader's familiarity both with the topic and the format of the text substantially influences his ability to understand. If the topic is very familiar, then he may have some difficulty but will probably be able to work through any problems. A child who knows about space exploration can often read new material about space missions even if the format isn't completely familiar.

If both the topic and format are unfamiliar, however, the reader is likely to have difficulty comprehending. This is why so many of us have trouble with, for example, income tax forms. We know little about the topic — we aren't familiar with the rules and regulations regarding taxes. In addition, we rarely read material that is structured like the tax forms and directions. Because both the topic and format are unfamiliar, we have trouble with this reading. Tax accountants, on the other hand, know the rules and regulations governing income taxes and, having read thousands of these forms and directions, are very familiar with their structure. Their familiarity with both the topic and format makes income tax forms very readable for them.

THE CONTEXT OF THE READING SITUATION

The context of the reading situation includes where the material is found, the physical location of the reader when reading, constraints imposed upon the reading, and the purpose for reading. For example, the same material found in a textbook, a newspaper, an advertisement, or a novel will not be read the same. In *Toward a Speech Act Theory of Literary Discourse*, Mary Louise Pratt says that readers have different expectations of various types of material and these expectations influence the reading process. For example, readers expect newspapers to be easy to read as well as biased. They expect novels to focus on human events in chronological order and to be enjoyable. They expect textbooks to contain lists of facts, have a categorical, logical organization, and to be boring and hard to read. Because of these expectations, readers approach various kinds of material differently.

The reader's physical location also makes a difference. In a study reported in *New Perspectives on Comprehension*, Jerome Harste and Robert Carey found that college students were more likely to identify the topic of an ambiguous text as wrestling when they were seated on a mat in a gym than when the same passage was read in an English class. The physical location itself appears to predispose our brains to make connections with certain past experiences. When in a gym, we activate experiences related to gyms in case they might be needed. The experiences activated might relate to the content, as in the case of the wrestling passage, or to the act of reading itself. Thus, a student who has experienced repeated failure in reading may begin a reading assignment in your class with a negative, self-defeating attitude. Why try, I'll only fail. I can't read, she may say to herself.

Aspects of the physical location affecting comfort also influence the reading process. Am I in a comfortable cozy chair or seated in a hard chair with my book on a desk? Is the room too cold or too warm? How much noise surrounds me?

The context can also constrain processing. In schools, teachers often impose constraints on processing by setting reading-related tasks. Requiring readers to answer questions at the end of a chapter, fill in worksheets, find definitions or make an outline focus attention on particular aspects of the text and suggest particular ways of reading. Students who are asked to fill in worksheets often avoid reading the entire text but skim to find the appropriate information. One student who received an A for her work in history confided that she completed an assignment to outline a chapter by copying from the text the title, major headings and sub-headings, and the first sentence of each paragraph. This was the extent of her reading.

The purpose for reading also forms part of the context of a situation. In *The Reader, the Text, the Poem*, Louise Rosenblatt indicates that stories are typically read for enjoyment, to experience a lived-through event, understand human characters and emotions, and recognize and appreciate the author's craft. Informational material, on the other hand, is usually read to garner important information about a topic.

These different purposes — reading for information and reading for pleasure — require different approaches to the act of reading. Rosenblatt makes it clear that the approach readers take is defined not by the nature of the text but by the purpose for reading. Any text can be read in any way. Stories can be read for information and informational material can be read for pleasure.

The tasks we impose on students in our classrooms often predispose them to read virtually everything for information. We ask them to identify main ideas and important details or we set purposes that focus attention on the information contained in a story or poem.

The purposes we set are often too narrow, focusing students' attention on a single aspect of a text while ignoring other important information. For example, if students are told to read to find out how plants with woody stems differ from those with green stems, they may do so — all the while failing to identify how these plants are alike.

Thus, when our assignments narrow the focus of reading, they may fail to help students understand how to vary their reading for different purposes. We need to help students understand how the process varies with changes in material, purpose, and context, and how they themselves affect the process. In addition, we need to provide opportunities for students to experience a variety of reading situations. In order to do this, we must know something about the reading process.

How Do We Read?

Reading is a process of constructing meaning in which the reader is an active participant. Meaning doesn't flow automatically from the text to the reader. Rather, the text contains clues that the reader uses to generate meaning.

To understand how this works, let's consider how we learn language. All our knowledge about language is based on our experiences. We develop concepts of "cat," "dog," "house," and everything else from our encounters with objects, people and events. Similarly, we develop our rules for behavior, including our rules for language, based on our experiences.

Our rules for behavior tell us how to dress for particular occasions — we don't usually wear evening gowns to the grocery store, for example — and our rules for language tell us the topics and language forms appropriate to given situations. Similarity in our experiences leads to similarity in our rule systems, and differences in our experiences lead to variations in our rules. For example, my rules for language may be similar to yours, but they will not be identical. My daughter's rules for language allow her to produce sentences like, "I'm fixin' to go to the store," while yours may lead you to produce, "I be goin' to the store," or "I say, I think I'll go to the store."

These differences mean that the rules an author uses to generate a text may not be the same as the rules a reader uses to generate meaning from the text. Because of differences in our language rules, meaning is never inherent in the words on the page. When authors compose, they embed in their texts many clues to their meaning. Text organization, vocabulary and sentence structure all provide clues, but it is the reader who gives meaning to the clues.

In an article in the *Journal of the Reading Specialist*, Kenneth Goodman describes reading as a process of predicting, gathering data, and confirming or disconfirming predictions. When encountering a text, readers use prior knowledge to predict what will be encountered. Predictions are made at many levels and can include predictions about the topic to be discussed, text organization, sentence structure and vocabulary. Even the next word or letter can be predicted. Then the reader samples the text, gathering information that can be used to confirm or disconfirm predictions.

In *The Foundations of Literacy*, Don Holdaway agrees with Goodman's description of the reading process. He emphasizes that the movement from surface language to meaning is personal and open to misinterpretation:

> Listeners and readers do not have the meanings poured into them — they are not conducted to them directly through the sounds in the air or from the marks on the paper; they make them from what is linguistically given in relationship to all that constitutes their own self-awareness. Thus, the interpretation of language is a creative process even when the most basic skills are being practiced.

The key to the entire process is that the reader is actively constructing meaning within the framework of a particular situational context. Of further importance is the role of prior knowledge in this process — as the source of predictions, as the basis for all reading behavior, and as the source of connections between new information and what is already known. Prior knowledge is important in so many ways that it needs additional discussion.

HOW DOES PRIOR KNOWLEDGE AFFECT READING?

When we encounter new objects, we use everything we've learned from our previous experiences to understand the new thing. We relate it to other similar-looking objects that might be found in a similar location or used for a similar task.

The same is true of reading. We use our past experiences with texts, language and human experiences to generate meaning from texts.

When I had difficulty with my son's science-fiction stories, for example, it was because I lacked previous experiences with this genre. I was unfamiliar with the way science fiction is organized, its vocabulary and unusual names. Most of all, however, it was the concepts or ideas that were strange to me. These stories included dreams that were reality and beings who communicated telepathically, entered the dreams of others and were capable of assuming spirit, human or other concrete forms. They included worlds where things were very different from the world I know — worlds where things were not what they seemed. The rules of human interaction and living that I had garnered from many years of experience simply did not apply to the worlds I encountered in these books.

This indicates the importance of prior knowledge in understanding any text. Readers need not know everything about a topic in order to understand, but they must have some knowledge that they can bring to bear on it. Students about to study photosynthesis might not know a great deal about it, but they probably know that plants need food and sunlight to grow and that leaves turn color in the fall. The less prior knowledge readers have to bring to bear on a new topic, the more difficult the reading will be.

It is not enough, however, to possess the knowledge; readers must also be able to draw on it. This is not simply a matter of remembering information. We often fail to use knowledge we possess because we don't view it as relevant. One of my favorite cartoons depicts a bird perched on top of a hippopotamus that is standing on the edge of a cliff. A nearby sign says,

Lovers' Leap. In the caption, the hippo is saying, "Wait just a darn minute; I just thought of something!" When I show this cartoon to people, at least half of them don't get the joke.

Several pieces of information are necessary to understand the cartoon. First, you must know what a lovers' leap is and that despondent lovers jump off lovers' leaps together. Then, you must infer that the bird and the hippo are lovers about to jump. Then, you must draw on your knowledge of birds and hippos — birds fly, hippos don't — to understand that if they jump, one of them will fly, but the other won't, a realization that was apparently just dawning on the hippo.

Most people to whom I've shown this cartoon possessed all the necessary information, but didn't activate it. Given the cartoon, it is difficult to know what information is relevant. Most people don't think about flying in relation to hippos. Thus, even proficient readers may not use the prior knowledge needed for understanding.

Fortunately, however, our prior knowledge is organized so that we can draw on it. Some people visualize this organization as a hierarchical filing system with items placed in files under major topics and subtopics. For example, information about birds might be in a file labeled Information about Animals located under Information about Living Things. To gain access to the information, we simply go to the right file in the right drawer in the right filing cabinet.

While this view is useful to a point, it fails to explain the connections readers make while reading. When reading a story about the death of a husband, what brings to mind the death of a grandfather or an uncle or son's recent auto accident? What causes me to substitute the word "luggage" for "language" when reading a book about children's language development while waiting for a plane in an airport? What brings to mind the sounds, smells and feelings related to other events when reading a novel? If prior knowledge is fragmented into compartments, how can one word or sentence evoke such a multitude of responses?

The answer is that prior knowledge is not stored in tidy compartments. Rather, it is organized in a complex, multi-dimensional arrangement of concepts. Because these concepts are interconnected, finding one item leads us to think about many other items related to the first. When sitting in an airport, for example, I activate, or bring to a conscious level, all my prior knowledge about airports including luggage, tickets, airplanes, my feelings about flying, my dislike of airplane food, memories of other flying experiences, and experiences related to flying like a movie I've seen, an article or story I've read, a cartoon about airline food, a friend who is a pilot, and so on. All these items are related not only to airports but also to other things like movies, mysteries, fears, friends, food and cartoons.

New information can be placed anywhere in the system. When this happens, it becomes part of a network that links it to other related items. It's the connections between the new information and the items already stored in prior knowledge that are vital. New information is connected to every item for which the reader can generate a connection.

It was my personal schema for airports or airplane trips that caused me to misread the word "language." My schema for airplane trips includes the items commonly associated with these trips as well as various related actions — buying a ticket, getting to the airport, checking in, boarding the plane, and so on. We develop schemata for things and events in our world, including baseball games, school, parties, novels, studying, stories, poems, cartoons and informational material. These schemata are generated from our experiences. Experiences attending school lead to the development of our school schema, experiences reading stories develop our schema for stories, and experiences with informational material develop our schema for expository texts.

If memory is stored in a multi-dimensional network, then what happens when we draw on prior knowledge for possible use? If we don't take out a file folder, then what do we do?

In a report titled *The Schema: A Structural or Functional Pattern?*, Iran Nejad-Asghar proposes a "light constellation" analogy to explain how memory works. He suggests that our cognitive network is like a bank of lights wired so that certain subsets of lights can be illuminated. For instance, all the blue lights could be lit or all the red ones, or a combination of blues and reds. Each subset of lights represents a schema. When a schema is activated, then that set of lights turns on. Of course, we are capable of illuminating more than one set of lights at any particular time. So, for example, when looking at the cartoon of the bird and the hippo, I can activate my schemata for both birds and hippos as well as my schema for cartoons.

But, if this is the case, why didn't my schema for hippos activate the knowledge, "cannot fly"? The activation process probably operates more like a dimmer than an on-off switch. That is, some items in the schema may shine more brightly than others. In the case of the cartoon, "cannot fly" is not brightly lit. On occasion, entire schemata may be more brightly lit than others.

When we read, appropriate schemata are activated. We link incoming information to information we already possess. First, we try to make these links to activated schemata. If no connection is possible, then other schemata may be searched and activated for likely connections. Because new "items" entered into the prior knowledge network include not only information but also relationships, the "new information" may simply involve creating new links among existing items. For example, the bird-hippo cartoon might cause me to connect birds and hippos in a new way. In this way, adding items to our store of prior knowledge can restructure the network.

Finally, we know that readers make inferences by generating new information based on information in the text. For example, if a story states that a mother is frowning and yelling at a child, the reader is likely to infer that the mother is angry. The reader has connected the stated information with previous information about mother-child relationships and generated new information or a new item in prior knowledge. As new items are added and new connections generated, the shape of prior knowledge changes constantly. The items remain, but the patterns shift, much like the patterns of a kaleidoscope.

Comprehension, then, depends on activating prior knowledge and developing links between new information and what is already known. In *Comprehension and Learning*, Frank Smith defines comprehension as "relating new experiences to the already known." Because prior knowledge is built from previous experiences, each individual's network is different. Therefore, teachers must help students activate their own prior knowledge and provide opportunities for them to relate new information to what is already known.

What Do Good Readers Do?

If we view reading as an active process, we can identify things proficient readers do when encountering texts. Proficient readers activate prior knowledge and connect new items to items in their store of prior knowledge. In addition, because they use prior knowledge to generate meaning from texts, they monitor their own understanding, focusing on meaning and checking themselves to see if they are understanding.

When they don't understand, they use a variety of strategies to achieve comprehension. For example, because I was monitoring my own reading, I stopped when I read "luggage" for "language" in the airport. The word "luggage" didn't make sense. My strategy was to reread that portion of the text.

Monitoring our understanding also keeps the reading process going when the meaning is not changed even though a reader may have substituted one word for another. The substitution of the word "house" for "home" in the sentence, "My home is in the city," would not cause a proficient reader to stop reading because the substitution doesn't affect the meaning. However, making the same substitution in the sentence, "I want to go home," would stop a reader who is monitoring for meaning.

Proficient readers use a variety of strategies to resolve a lack of understanding. They may go back and reread, as I did, or continue reading to gather additional information. They may use their knowledge of sound-symbol relationships to sound out a problematic word or they may check for meaning with an outside source such as a dictionary, encyclopedia, teacher, parent or friend. If entire texts are giving them difficulty, they may read alternative texts or seek help from an expert or friend.

What Do We Know about Learning That Can Help Us?

Teaching in general, and reading instruction in particular, have been strongly criticized in recent years. Critics say that we aren't teaching students to think and that, in fact, instructional methods actually prevent students from engaging in critical thinking.

In *Learning Strategies*, Don Dansereau suggests that "teaching and testing methods implicitly encourage rote memorization by specifying exactly what must be learned, rewarding verbatim answers on tests and putting little emphasis on the development of relationships between incoming and stored information." In an article in *Secondary School Reading*, Sharon Pugh Smith, Robert Carey and Jerome Harste indicate that some students "may become so dependent on teacher organization of meaning that they may have difficulty learning to learn for themselves after high school." And, in an article in *The Reading Teacher*, Gerry Duffy and Kathy Roehler contend that "students learn isolated exercises that have little to do with making sense out of a text." These are only a few of the critiques that maintain that teachers place too much emphasis on learning isolated facts through memorization and engaging in isolated exercises.

In addition, by engaging in this kind of instruction, we take responsibility for students' understanding of text material and learning of course content. How do we do so?

— By giving students graphic organizers that show them the important information and the organizational structure of the text.
— By giving them worksheets that identify important information and then going over the worksheets in class to make sure that everyone has the same right answer.
— By lecturing on the material in the text to make sure that everyone understands it.
— By reviewing material that will be on tests.
— By giving tests that focus on reiterating specific information.

We often do these things for very good reasons—we want students to learn the specific information we are teaching. However, we must also recognize that these activities, and others like them, don't help students learn or think, nor do they help students become learners. True learning takes place when new information is integrated into our prior knowledge by linking it to known information. Connections and relationships with other concepts in our cognitive system must be developed, and only the learner can develop those connections. Typical instructional activities, like those listed previously, don't help students make connections between the new and their own prior knowledge. Students memorize instead of learn, and when the test is over, they promptly forget the new information.

As Jerome Bruner noted in *Actual Minds, Possible Worlds*, teachers can close down what he called the "process of wondering" or open it up. In other words, teachers can do much to help students become active, thoughtful learners. More than ten years ago, Rob Tierney and P. David Pearson suggested that teachers need to:

— Recognize that reading is interactive and, thus, readers have a right to interpret texts.
— Encourage students to tie information to prior knowledge.
— Give students opportunities to evaluate their interpretations.

Most of us have yet to allow or encourage these activities in our classrooms. In *New Policy Guidelines in Reading: Connecting Research and Practice*, Jerome Harste says that learning a process requires three things—engaging in the process, being with others engaged in the process, and bringing aspects of the process to a conscious level. This means that, rather than simply memorizing, students must actively engage in learning in an environment that encourages them to take risks and engage in meaningful activities that reflect real-world activities. They must also have opportunities to talk to other learners about what—and how—they are learning.

EMPOWERMENT AND ACTIVE ENGAGEMENT

Students are often depicted as sponges soaking up information from textbooks and teachers, then retrieving that information on demand to answer teachers' questions orally or in writing on tests and worksheets. In this scenario, the teacher's job is to provide the information that soaks into the sponges.

This analogy suggests that students are passive recipients of whatever is presented to them, and that teaching is simply a matter of presenting information.

Additionally, if we extend the analogy, we're likely to come across some things that we haven't considered about sponges. For example, they won't soak up powders, such as sugar and flour, solids, such as a block of cheese or a slice of bread, and semi-liquids, such as jams and jellies. Sponges reject material that doesn't suit them. If students are like sponges, they too may reject material that doesn't suit them. Our task as teachers, then, would involve identifying materials students will accept, while ignoring everything else.

Further, if sponges are left unattended, the fluids they have soaked up evaporate and they dry out. Continuing the analogy, then, we would expect information that we have poured into students to evaporate and disappear. Yet teachers don't expect students to forget everything they've been taught. If this were so, schools would be useless.

In fact, students are not like sponges. They are active learners, even when they seem most passive. In *Comprehension and Learning*, Frank Smith says that students are always learning; they just may not be learning what we expect them to learn. Learning is not a matter of taking in new information and adding it to our current store of knowledge. In order for new information to be added to our cognitive network, it must be linked to what is already there. This generates a rearrangement of the cognitive network to accommodate the new. Thus, learning involves changing or elaborating on what is already known.

The only person who can attach the new to what is already known or who can change the current arrangement of information is the learner. Teachers can do things to help the learner with this task, but we cannot do it *for* the learner.

Learners will not engage in the task of cognitive restructuring unless they are in a situation that encourages them to do so. If their only task is to reiterate information presented by the teacher, then they will make little or no attempt to incorporate the information into their store of knowledge. If the teacher does all the thinking for students, then there is no need for them to think for themselves. To maintain active learning, we must empower students — help them take charge of their own learning.

This doesn't mean that we should never do things that help students understand text material. Infotexts often do a poor job of presenting complex concepts, and there is much that teachers can do that does not entail assuming the responsibility for learning. Films that help students understand historical settings and events, demonstrations and activities that expand ideas and explain concepts, and lectures that provide additional information or explanation are all helpful. The key is that these activities encourage students to maintain control of their own learning.

In addition, we must also do things to help students learn how to take charge of their learning. Students have often become so used to teachers doing everything for them that they don't know how to do things for themselves. The grade the teacher puts on their worksheet tells them whether they have understood the chapter. Without the grade, they don't know how to tell whether they've understood. Further, they often don't know how to monitor their own learning or what to do when they don't understand. We must engage students in activities that help them both take charge of and monitor their learning.

Donald Graves and Lucy Calkins have pointed out the importance of ownership in learning to write and Jeanne Harms and Lucille Lettow point out the importance of ownership in learning to read. But ownership — being in charge of our own learning process — is important in all aspects of learning.

Ownership, or empowerment, involves making choices and teachers are often wary of this. Perhaps we are concerned that if students are allowed choice, they may choose not to learn or they may choose not to learn what we want them to learn. For some, providing choices implies that there will be chaos in the classroom.

Providing choices, however, doesn't mean that teachers must relinquish their role. It simply means giving students options within a larger framework. For example, students may have no choice about whether they will study ancient Greece. However, during the unit, they may be encouraged to choose both to study a specific aspect of ancient Greece and the other students they will work with. While all the groups may be expected to present what they've learned to the class, they may choose the format of their presentation. Thus, providing choices doesn't place students in charge of the class — it means that teachers and students work together to learn and, during that process, determine curriculum.

When students are in control of their own learning, they are more likely to become actively involved in learning. They actively determine the importance of various items of information, the relationships between new information and their own lives, and how the information can be used.

PROVIDING A LOW-RISK ENVIRONMENT

For students to take advantage of choice, they must be in a low-risk environment; that is, they must be in a situation where they are not penalized for the choices they make or the chances they take with learning. If, for example, they are penalized for making mistakes when they are first learning to read or write, they are likely to become very cautious about reading and writing.

In high-risk situations where writing is expected to be conventional in every way, young writers will likely write only words they know how to spell and sentences they know are "correct." Some children who come to believe that they can never produce "correct" writing opt out and stop writing entirely.

Students need to be in low-risk situations for all learning. We need to recognize that making mistakes is a natural part of learning and encourage students to explore new ideas and topics without fear of being penalized for their explorations.

Instructional strategies that escalate risk can take many forms, but are most often found in activities, worksheets and tests that focus on a single right answer that will be marked. When grades are being given, students are very careful about what they produce. If high grades depend upon producing certain information or demonstrating competence with certain skills, then students will comply. And, if the teacher is responsible for handing out the grades, students will change their behavior in the presence of the teacher.

In *From Communication to Curriculum*, Douglas Barnes reported his observations that students working in small groups who had been engaged in "exploratory" talk shifted to "performance" language when the teacher joined the group. They moved from talking about possible explanations and evaluating those possibilities to demonstrating for the teacher what they knew. When the teacher was not part of the group, students talked to each other, but when the teacher joined the group, everyone talked to the teacher.

We can probably never create a no-risk situation, but we can reduce the risk level by encouraging students to explore, valuing them and the work they produce, accepting mistakes as a natural part of learning, and learning with them.

In our investigation of social studies classrooms, Fred Smith and I found that classroom reading activities bore little resemblance to reading in the real world. In the real world, people read for real purposes and choose materials that meet their needs. Once gained, information is evaluated and compared to other information, then used in some way. In the schools studied, students read because they were told to, they had no choice in the material read, and they used the information only to answer questions on worksheets and tests. In addition, the material covered rarely related to their lives outside school. These students were not engaged in meaningful activities, nor did the activities or materials reflect the world outside school.

Meaningful activities are similar to those students would be engaged in if they weren't in school. They involve the students in the kinds of thinking, writing, reading and discussing that go on in the real world. They also encourage learners to make choices and place them in charge of their own learning.

"Talking enables us to rearrange the problem so that we can look at it differently," Douglas Barnes said in his discussion of the advantages of group talk. He is not alone in this view. In *Thought and Language*, Lev Vygotsky said that language is the vehicle for thinking and, in *Actual Minds, Possible Worlds*, Jerome Bruner expressed his belief that growth occurs through recording information in new forms.

Listening to others' views of something we have all read increases our understanding of a text because we come to view it from many perspectives. Working with others to solve problems or explore ideas produces talk that allows everyone involved to expand their thinking.

Collaboration—students working together to decide what and how to study, investigate topics, discuss information and ideas, and plan how to share information with others—is invaluable. In contrast to cooperative activities—in which all students complete one part of a task often assigned by the teacher—collaboration involves all students in working together. While the general task, such as studying a European country or determining what happened and why during a science experiment, may be assigned by the teacher, the teacher doesn't assign specific tasks to particular students.

Collaboration provides students with access to others' thoughts, interpretations of material, and questions. Because this approach encourages students to check their own understanding against that of others, they can both monitor and expand their understanding. While a teacher's questions often identify for students items the teacher considers important, this is not as effective as encouraging students to compare their own understanding with that of other students. During a discussion, they have an opportunity to express and explain their own understanding and question others about theirs. When only the teacher asks the questions, the answers expected are often either right or wrong and there is little opportunity for students to question what is presented.

Collaboration also helps establish a low-risk situation. When a single student works on a task or answers a question, he or she alone is totally responsible for the work. This increases the risk involved. However, in a collaborative situation, students share responsibility. There is no attempt to identify who is right or wrong. They simply discuss the material read to reach agreement about what it means or work on a task together, sharing responsibility for the product.

Summary

If students are to learn the content we want them to learn, we must help them become actively engaged in their own learning. In so doing, we can also help them understand the reading process and become effective readers, thinkers and learners.

The remainder of this book outlines strategies to help ensure that students learn *through* reading as well as *about* reading.

EVALUATING STUDENTS –

AND TEXTS

Only when we know the strengths and weaknesses of both the students and the texts they will encounter can we plan instruction to help students cope with the material. This chapter will look at methods of evaluating students' reading ability and determining the strengths and weaknesses of the texts we use.

What Should We Evaluate and Why?

John: Science and social studies books are harder to read than stories. My third-graders can understand stories, but not informational material.

Mary: My ninth-graders have the same problem. They can't read their science and history books.

John: That's because stories are easier to read than books about science, history, math and things like that.

Louise: Wait a minute, John, don't your eight-year-olds read lots of books about dinosaurs? And, Mary, don't your ninth-graders read everything they can find about earthquakes and volcanoes?

John: But that's different—those are just stories about dinosaurs.

This conversation is, of course, fictitious, but the ideas expressed by John and Mary are real in that they reflect two commonly held beliefs:

— Stories are easier to read than informational material.

— Children can read and understand stories at a young age but can read and understand informational material only much later.

These assumptions have influenced instruction and material for many years. They pervade the work of developmental theorists, such as James Britton, Tony Burgess, Nancy Martin, Alex McLeod, and Harold Rosen and James Moffett. Research studies, such as those of Suzanne Hidi and Angela Hildyard and Judith Langer, that suggest that older students have more difficulty with non-fiction than with fiction also reinforce these ideas. Overall, there has been strong support for the belief that children cannot cope with the logical organization, complex sentence structures or abstract concepts associated with informational texts.

Because fiction is considered easier to read, basal readers have traditionally included stories and an occasional poem. Although this has begun to change in recent years so that there is now greater variety in these readers, stories continue to predominate. Many infotexts, especially those designed for young readers, are written in a narrative style in the belief that this will make them more like fiction, improving their readability. Social studies texts, in particular, often use this ploy. For example, a family—usually a father, mother, boy and girl—takes a trip somewhere, like France, and information about France is integrated into the story of the family's travels.

All this has led to a focus on fiction in elementary schools, where children have many experiences with both reading and writing stories. By the time they enter third or fourth grade, they are familiar with the structures, coherence patterns, vocabulary, topics, and other features of narrative texts.

On the other hand, because they have read—and been expected to write—little in the way of informational material, they are often unfamiliar with the structures, patterns, vocabulary, and other features of this kind of text. It is this unfamiliarity, rather than any inherent developmental shortcoming in the reader, that makes informational material difficult.

Whether it is fiction or non-fiction designed to read like fiction, text written in a narrative style is different from expository writing. In an article in *Journal of Reading*, Carolyn Kent, for example, says that narratives have a first- or third-person point of view; that is, the story is told by one of the characters or an outside narrator. The reader determines who is telling the story and develops expectations based on this point of view. The point of view of writers of expository material is less easily identified.

Narratives are agent-oriented in that they focus on one or more characters. This focus is familiar because our lives involve relationships and interactions with others. Narrative-style texts are familiar because they build on these. Expository texts, on the other hand, focus on topics or subject matter. Except in school situations, our conversations focus on these far less frequently. For this reason, students are far less familiar with discussions, both oral and written, that involve the transmission of information.

Finally, the events of stories occur in a time frame and are linked chronologically. Expository material, on the other hand, has no temporal focus — time is not important because the information is considered timeless. Information is connected using techniques such as making comparisons, supporting main ideas with details, and citing examples to illustrate concepts.

The differences between expository and narrative texts, as well as students' previous experiences with informational material should be considered when deciding whether a text is likely to be readable. Because students' previous experience affects their reading, we must determine each individual's ability to read a particular text. This decision can't be made on the basis of their performance on general reading tests, which tell us only whether they can read and understand the passages selected for inclusion in the test. Nor can it be made based on applying readability formulas to a particular text. Again, students' ability to read the text will depend on their prior knowledge.

To determine whether students can read a particular text, we must examine both the students to determine their familiarity with the features of a particular text and the text to determine features that may create difficulties for the students.

Evaluating Students

One of the best ways of determining whether students are able to read a particular text is to use a content informal reading inventory. At best, general reading tests indicate only that students can read the passages found on the test and answer the questions that accompany them. These passages may not represent the kind of material students are required to read in class and the questions may not require the kinds of thinking and reading we want to encourage.

Because a content informal reading inventory uses texts and questions selected by the teacher, it provides direct information about students' ability to read a particular passage. An advantage of an IRI is that it can be given to an entire class during a single class period. It's worth noting, however, that we can learn much more about students if the inventory is administered individually. Although it takes longer, this allows us to discuss answers with individual students, providing better information about their reading strategies. Because of time constraints, it may be useful to test an entire class, then administer individual IRIs to selected students.

For an IRI, students read a passage from a text they will be required to read and answer questions created by the teacher. When selecting the passage, several factors should be considered. First, it should be a complete unit, such as a section or sub-section of a chapter, that makes sense when it stands alone. A passage that is incomplete will leave readers frustrated and unable to comprehend major points or make inferences.

Second, select a passage that is representative of the entire text. Material from the first chapter of a text and passages from the beginning of other chapters are not usually good choices because, as introductions, they tend to be general in nature and unrepresentative of the balance of the text.

Third, the passage needs to be long enough to provide a good estimate of students' ability. Short passages don't provide enough information for students to begin to engage in proficient reading. Nor do they provide enough information or depth for the teacher to evaluate students' ability to think critically. In addition, the passage should be long enough to provide material for generating ten to fifteen questions, but short enough for students to read it and answer the questions in one class period. The length may vary from 250 words for eight-year-olds to 1,000 words for high school students.

Once the passage is selected, create ten to fifteen questions related to it. Questions usually evaluate several aspects of comprehension:

— Ability to understand vocabulary.
— Ability to recall details.
— Ability to identify or generate main ideas.
— Ability to make inferences.
— Ability to apply what has been learned.

To obtain the best information about students, the questions should be inter-related and presented in a logical order. Asking unrelated questions will reveal whether students can answer certain kinds of questions, but will tell us nothing about their thinking ability. Inter-related questions, on the other hand, provide us with insights into students' problems. For example, if students can answer questions requiring them to recall details and make inferences, but not those requiring them to apply this information, then they may need help in this area.

Here is a series of IRI questions created to accompany a passage about ancient Greece:

1. What was the form of government in Athens?
2. How much freedom did the common person have in Athens?
3. How did Athenians feel about education and what was the focus of that education?
4. What form of government did Sparta have?
5. How much freedom did the common person have in Sparta?
6. What was the focus of education in Sparta?
7. What single word best describes Sparta?
8. What single word best describes Athens?
9. "Sparta is the best place to live." Agree or disagree with this statement and give reasons.
10. "Athens is the best place to live." Agree or disagree with this statement and give reasons.

11. Would you rather live in Sparta or Athens? Give reasons for your answer.

The first eight questions require students to recall details. The ninth and tenth require them to make inferences and the eleventh requires them to apply the information gathered from the reading. The final three questions relate directly to the earlier questions because the details recalled in the first eight provide the basis for the answers to the ninth, tenth and eleventh. Students who can answer the detail questions but not the inference questions may be having difficulty making inferences. If they can't answer the application question, it's worth looking to see if they have correctly answered the inference and detail questions.

ALTERNATIVE METHODS OF EVALUATING READING ABILITY

Perhaps the most straightforward method is simply to ask students whether material is too easy, about right, or too difficult. Talk to them about what makes the text easy or difficult to read.

An alternative is to present students with texts at three different levels and ask them to identify which is the easiest and which the most difficult to understand. Discuss the reasons for their choices.

Another possibility is to monitor students' reading. While students are reading silently, sit next to one and ask her or him to read aloud quietly part of the text or tell you about the chapter. You might also ask a few specific questions of your own. Only four or five minutes are needed to determine whether a student is understanding the text at that point. Over a period of several weeks, each student in the class can be evaluated in this way.

Finally, the best way to make sure that students are reading infotexts that are "right" for them is to encourage them to select their own material. This requires that a variety of books on a topic be available. These books should vary in difficulty and present the information in a variety of formats. Students can read one or more books to gather information about the topic, selecting material appropriate for their own reading level.

Evaluating Texts

Readability formulas are commonly used to determine the reading level of texts. The assumption is that if a readability formula is used to determine the reading level of a text and a reading test is used to determine the reading level of a student, student and text can be appropriately matched. For instance, a student reading at a grade-four level can be placed in a text that has a fourth-grade readability rating.

There are two problems with this. First, reading tests are not necessarily an accurate gauge of students' reading ability and, even if they were, these tests don't indicate how well a student will be able to read a specific text that may have features different from the passages on the reading test.

Second, readability formulas, by and large, evaluate only two aspects of texts—vocabulary and syntactic complexity. Vocabulary difficulty is typically measured on the assumption that long words are harder to understand than short. The more syllables in a word, the more difficult it is considered. This approach does not take into account readers' previous experience. Words like "mitosis," "cognitive," and "decadence" may be more difficult for young children to read and understand than "dog," "cat," and "ran," but these same children can understand many long words such as "dinosaur," "hamburger," "reptile," and "computer" because they are part of their experience. At the same time, many short words like "id," "quark" and "ego" present problems even for proficient readers. Assessing words on the basis of their length or, in some cases, whether they appear on basic word lists doesn't take into account the potential prior knowledge of the reader.

Syntactic complexity is also commonly measured on the assumption that long sentences are more difficult to read than short. We've all encountered sentences that are so long that we have difficulty figuring out the point. Our difficulty probably stems from the fact that we are unfamiliar with over-long sentences because they occur so rarely.

Short sentences, too, can pose problems for readers because they chop up meaning and fail to provide essential clues about relationships among ideas. Consider the following sentences, for example: "The cotton gin was invented. More slaves were needed to pick cotton. The cotton gin could gin more cotton than people could." In the absence of clues about the relationship between the invention of the cotton gin and the need for more slaves, readers are left to infer these connections. As an adult, I might question why having a cotton gin that could gin a lot of cotton would increase the demand for slaves. Younger readers, however, might not even search for a connection among these ideas.

In an essay in *Theoretical Models and Processes of Reading*, P. David Pearson reported the results of his study of young children's ability to read syntactically complex sentences. He found that children read and recalled longer, complex sentences better than short, simple ones. The additional information in the more complex sentences provided clues that enabled readers to comprehend and recall. As Jerome Harste, Virginia Woodward and Carolyn Burke suggest in their book, *Language Stories and Literacy Lessons*, simplicity deprives language users of support for understanding while complexity supports understanding.

While teachers may find readability formulas useful for obtaining a general idea of the suitability of a text for a particular class, those who know their students can usually determine a book's suitability by simply reading portions of the text. Other methods of evaluating texts are often more useful than using readability formulas.

READER-FRIENDLINESS

Rather than relying on formulas, it's more useful to consider specific factors that make a text more or less readable. In an article in *Journal of Reading*, Judith Irwin and Carol Davis proposed criteria for evaluating the qualities of infotexts. Their checklist analyzes three things: understandability, learnability and readability. When analyzing understandability, they suggest that teachers consider the prior knowledge of students with respect to vocabulary, new concepts, abstract concepts and sentence complexity, and evaluate how the text presents vocabulary, new concepts and abstract concepts as well as statements of main ideas and complex relationships.

Analyzing learnability includes considering the organization of the text, and the level of reinforcement and motivation it provides. Organization encompasses the organization of chapters, the presence of aids such as an index, glossary and table of contents, and the relationship between questions and the information in and organization of chapters. Reinforcement refers to the presence of opportunities for students to practice using new concepts — does the text include summaries, aids such as maps and graphs, supplementary activities designed to accommodate a broad range of ability levels, and questions that require students to recall details, make inferences and think creatively? In addition to the appearance of the text — format, print size and illustrations as well as titles, headings and subheadings — motivation encompasses the writing style, whether activities are motivating, how information is applied, and whether there is an appropriate gender, racial and cultural mix.

The final section of the checklist, the readability analysis, consists of a series of questions designed to help the evaluator consider the responses to questions in the other categories. The evaluator is asked to compare weaknesses and strengths and to think about instruction that will take advantage of the assets of the text.

Checklists like this can help identify criteria for evaluating a complete text as long as we keep in mind that not all texts contain, or should contain, all the features outlined. They are useful when deciding which texts to use or in alerting us to problems with specific texts. As an overall evaluation of the merits of a text, they provide a reasonable alternative to applying a readability formula because they provide specific information about the text. On the other hand, they don't provide information about specific material that may be useful when planning daily instruction.

EVALUATION FOR INSTRUCTIONAL PLANNING

Within texts, the readability of individual chapters and, indeed, specific passages within those chapters may vary greatly. In addition to assessing the overall merits of a text, we need to examine the specific material we are requiring students to read to identify strengths that can be used to advantage and weaknesses that may cause difficulties. Then we can plan instruction, provide material and create situations to compensate for textual shortcomings.

The criteria outlined in this section were identified by teachers and education students as they evaluated a variety of infotexts and planned instruction based on their findings. The criteria are broad enough to be used successfully with a variety of texts—math, science, social studies, health, computer science, etc. Although these teachers were not familiar with the checklist outlined in the previous section, some of the criteria are remarkably similar to those suggested by Irwin and Davis.

Information

There are many factors to consider when evaluating the information in a text. One is the concept load—how many new concepts are presented and how quickly? For instance, a single ten-page chapter may introduce ten new concepts—one on each page. On the other hand, the chapter may load five new concepts onto one page, three onto another, two onto another and none onto the remaining pages. While the total number of new concepts introduced may not be unreasonable, the density of concepts presented in particular sections may pose problems.

Depth is a second consideration—does the chapter discuss each concept in depth or does it suffer from what Harriet Bernstein identifies as "mentioning"? Mentioning occurs when texts present many items of information but discuss few, if any, of them in depth.

Consider, for example, this brief text: "Spiders can be large or small. Spiders make webs. Spiders catch food in their webs." Several facts about spiders are mentioned, but none is discussed in detail. The same problem often plagues longer texts, causing misunderstandings by students. For example, one social studies text dealt with the underground railroad in two sentences. The first said the underground railroad was a system for transporting slaves to the North and to Canada. The second said that the system consisted of "stations" where people could rest and be fed. The ten- and eleven-year-old students who read this concluded that the underground railroad was a subway system.

This problem often results from attempting to cover too much material in a single text or in a single chapter. In some textbooks, World War I, ancient Greece, energy and the human skeleton are covered in single chapters varying in length from ten to fifteen pages, including illustrations. The result is that very little can be covered in any depth.

A third consideration is whether the information presented is relevant. Mentioning items without providing depth can sometimes make relevant information appear irrelevant because its relationship to other information is not clear. On the other hand, irrelevant information is sometimes included while information that ought to be included is omitted. One American history text detailed the life histories of two people involved in the American Civil War—Abraham Lincoln and Robert E. Lee—providing information about their births and childhoods that had no connection to the topic of the chapter. At the same time, the text devoted only one sentence each to the president of the Southern States, Jefferson Davis, and the Northern general, Ulysses S. Grant.

It is critical to ask whether relationships among ideas are made clear or if the reader must infer the connections. The passage about the cotton gin quoted earlier is an example of a text that doesn't clarify the relationships among ideas and so appears to suffer from "mentioning."

Finally, we must decide whether ideas are presented in a way that is relevant to students. Information they consider irrelevant will bore them and will, at best, be memorized for a test, then forgotten. This doesn't mean that we must eliminate certain topics from our course of instruction; it does mean that topics need to be presented so that students can make connections between their own lives and what is presented in the text. The best texts are written with the intended audience, and the interests of that audience, in mind.

Vocabulary

When considering vocabulary, it's important to keep in mind students' prior knowledge: what do they already know about the topic? Many texts list new vocabulary at the beginning or end of chapters, identify it in bold print in the body of the text, or supply definitions in the margins. Check these words, asking if they are unfamiliar to students. Next, ask if the definitions and explanations provided are adequate. An explanation that says, "Mechanical energy is a form of kinetic energy," does little to enhance our understanding of mechanical energy. New terms, which are really new concepts, are often defined in a single sentence. Check to see if there are additional explanations or if examples are provided to help students understand the new vocabulary—and thus new concepts.

When reading a chapter, look for words not identified as new vocabulary that might be unfamiliar to the students. The writer may be making invalid assumptions about students' prior knowledge. Are there terms that ought to be defined but aren't? Is there sufficient context for students to determine the meaning of these words?

Organization

Organization refers to the overall structure of a chapter as well as the sub-units within it—paragraphs, sub-sections and sections. Is the chapter organized in a recognizable way? Is the organization obvious and keyed to the headings and sub-headings?

The organization of the chapter on the American Civil War referred to earlier was flawed because events were not presented in sequence. The time frame jumped from before the war to during the war and then back to a discussion of pre-war issues.

In addition, the relationship between headings and sub-headings should be evaluated. Do they fit logically? A major section of the chapter on the American Civil War, for example, was headed, "Problems That Led Up to the War." The sub-headings were, "Problems With Slavery," "Problems With Taxes" and "Three Black Leaders." The last has no apparent connection either to the first two headings or to the main heading. Because headings and subheadings provide organizational pointers, unrelated headings can create difficulties for students.

Another factor contributing to the logical structure of a chapter is the organization of sub-sections—do the paragraphs in a sub-section fit logically and do the subheadings reflect the relationships among the paragraphs? A chapter about China in a social studies text, for example, included a sub-section titled "Mongolia." It contained five paragraphs, two on Inner Mongolia, two on Outer Mongolia and one on Tibet. The rationale for including information about Tibet in the text, while failing to mention it in the subheading, wasn't explained. Problems like this create major difficulties for students who use textual clues to determine structure and identify important information.

We must also ask ourselves whether main ideas are stated and, perhaps more important, whether the text is organized around main ideas. We often assume that paragraphs contain main ideas when, in fact, they frequently don't. In an article in *Journal of Reading Behavior*, Jim Baumann and Judith Serra analyzed the social studies texts of five major publishers to determine whether main ideas were present. They found that only 27 per cent of the passages contained explicitly stated main ideas. Paragraphs often consist of a collection of facts that have a general relationship—they may all be about the Industrial Revolution, for example—but each is about a different item.

Further, we must examine whether the paragraphs in a sub-section are related and whether the sentences in paragraphs are related. Individual sentences often seem to stand alone, making the paragraph seem more like a list of information than a paragraph. Similarly, the paragraphs in a sub-section may seem independent of other paragraphs. The paragraph on Tibet mentioned earlier is an example of this. A list of unrelated information is more difficult to understand and remember than information presented in an organized manner. Passages may appear to be organized in paragraphs when, in fact, the logical organization of paragraphs is absent. This places readers at a disadvantage.

Finally, we must consider sentences—are they so long that readers become lost in the wording or so short that they interfere with the flow of ideas? We might also ask if students are likely to find the structures familiar or are there unusual constructions that will be puzzling.

Graphics

Because graphics—illustrations, charts, maps, photographs and anything that relates to the appearance of the text on the page—are important features of infotexts, we must examine both their usefulness and relevance. Is a particular map helpful in understanding the text? Does a picture illustrate the information contained in a math problem? Does a photograph of a solar house help students understand solar energy?

While graphics may be eye-catching, they should also be helpful. For example, close examination of some very colorful and attractive illustrations in a chapter in a math text revealed that they were totally unrelated to the material on the page.

In addition, the graphics should be understandable. One history chapter contained maps that might have been useful if they hadn't been so crammed with information that they became confusing and unreadable. A chapter on ratios in a math book asked students to compare the size of real animals and toy animals. However, the real animals and toy animals shown in the accompanying pictures were the same size, suggesting that there are no differences.

Illustrations can enhance understanding by providing information that running text cannot, such as photographs of living conditions, maps of areas, and diagrams of the human body. They do this, however, only if they are clear, understandable and related to the concepts discussed in the text.

The position of graphics also influences their effectiveness. They should, for example, be placed on the same page as the related print information. Readers should not be required to flip pages in order to view illustrations.

Finally, we must consider the appearance of the text itself. Is it pleasing to the eye? While print need not be large, very small type can be hard to read for an extended period. And pages that present an overwhelming amount of dense print may discourage readers before they even begin. Further, headings, subheadings, vocabulary, important concepts, and other items should by readily distinguished by, for example, boldface type.

Questions

Many textbooks include a series of questions at the ends of chapters that should be examined carefully before they are presented to students.

Unfortunately, answering these questions sometimes requires information that wasn't provided in the chapter. The writer assumes that students will be able to generate an answer by combining facts outlined in the chapter with their own prior knowledge. However, students often do not possess the prior knowledge required.

Questions should also focus on the most important information in the chapter, not on irrelevant details. While it is logical to expect questions to be designed to reinforce the most important information, this is often not the case. In fact, they often focus on unimportant details.

We must also evaluate whether readers will be able to understand what the questions are asking. If they can't understand the question, they can't answer it.

Finally, it's a good idea to identify the kinds of thinking required by the questions. Do they focus on minor or major details? Do they ask about main ideas or major concepts? Do they require students to make inferences or apply information? Good questions should do all this.

Other Supplemental Aids

Does the chapter contain supplemental aids — an introduction, graphic organizers, definitions in the margins of the text, a summary — that support readers? These aids help readers understand the organization of the chapter as well as the content. Aids such as a list of additional resources can provide students with alternative texts if they are having trouble with the one they are reading. These aids are not absolutely necessary — many texts are readable and understandable without them — nor will they, on their own, salvage a text that is riddled with other problems. Nevertheless, they do help readers and are an asset to any chapter.

Bias

It is important to identify the biases in infotexts. The central issue is not whether a text is biased — all texts are — but what the biases are. Because the bias may be very subtle, it is not always easy to detect. For example, a photograph included in the previously mentioned chapter on the American Civil War showed African-American men elected to Congress during the reconstruction period after the war. On the surface, this seems like an attempt to present a positive view of African-Americans. However, the caption simply indicated that black men were elected to Congress after the war and failed to name any of the men pictured or indicate the states they represented.

Look for balance in representations of gender as well as ethnic origin. A math book that uses illustrations of females for problems involving cooking and males for those involving building and scientific endeavors promotes sexual stereotypes. Finally, examine texts to ensure that they reflect the cultural diversity of the communities in which they are used.

Summary

Evaluating students and texts provides the information needed to develop an effective program. Knowing students' weaknesses allows us to plan instruction to help overcome their difficulties and identifying the shortcomings of texts allows us to plan instruction to compensates for these and help students develop strategies for coping with them.

Considering each of these factors when reading a text may seem like an overwhelming task. Initially, you may decide to limit your evaluation to only a few factors, expanding your criteria as you become comfortable with the process. If you put yourself in the students' shoes and read from their perspective, you'll find yourself recognizing both features that aid the reader and those likely to create difficulties. This will take some time at first but, as you become familiar with viewing texts from this perspective, you'll begin to notice more.

. . . .

MAKING CONNECTIONS

We learn by linking new information to what we already know. All day, every day, we make sense of our world by comparing the things we encounter with our current understanding. In *Comprehension and Learning*, Frank Smith calls this understanding our "theory of the world in our heads."

Based on our experiences, Smith says, we build a set of concepts, or rules, that explain how the world around us works, then use these rules to make decisions about our behavior. For example, our rules tell us how to dress for a picnic at the beach, a formal dinner party or a trip to the supermarket. These rules are both sociocentric and idiocentric — while they are certainly influenced by the community in which we live, they are also particular to each of us as individuals. For example, although my teenaged daughter and I may dress quite differently for a trip to the supermarket because our idiocentric rules are different, neither of us is likely to wear a nightgown, swimsuit or formal gown because our sociocentric rules are similar.

These rules change as needed. They aren't so much a list of dos and don'ts as parameters that describe and define our world. We use these parameters, which define our individual schemata, to make sense of new things as we encounter them. If we see a strange animal, for example, we compare it to animals we already know about to determine what it may be and how it might act. In the same way, when we encounter a new situation, we compare it to familiar situations before deciding how to act.

When they encounter new information in the books, films and classroom lectures that are a normal part of schooling, students do the same thing — they use what they already know to make sense of the new. This means that students' prior knowledge is very important. They understand new information only by using what they already know. If they are from the same community, their previous experiences — and thus their prior knowledge — are probably similar. However, there will also be differences in their prior knowledge because at least some of their experiences will have been different and their personal behavioral schemata are idiocentric as well as sociocentric.

While all students possess prior knowledge, this may not include the specific knowledge or experiences likely to help them understand a topic of study. And, even if they do possess the necessary knowledge, they may be unable to draw on this information to help them understand the specific material they encounter. If we want students to truly understand what we are teaching, we must help them use the information they already possess. And, if we find that they lack pertinent information, we must provide bridges between what they already know and what they will encounter in our classes.

Finding Out What Students Know

PRE-TESTS

Pre-tests are often used to discover the extent of students' prior knowledge of a topic. Typically, they involve creating a test similar to one that might be given at the end of a unit and administering it before the unit begins. While this will reveal what students already know about the specific questions asked, it won't tell us what else students know about the topic. In addition, because pre-tests focus on what will be taught, they don't reveal much about students' previous experiences.

Despite their drawbacks, pre-tests can be very helpful. For example, if I were going to teach a math unit on division, I might create a test consisting of division problems to find out who already knows how to do this. I might also give a test consisting of multiplication, addition, and subtraction problems because knowing these procedures is helpful when doing division.

While pre-tests help teachers find out what students know about specific topics, they also help students identify the specific information to be covered. However, they do not help students make connections with their prior knowledge.

TERMINOLOGY LISTS

Lists of terminology students are likely to encounter when studying a topic can also provide a useful indication of the extent of their prior knowledge.

Develop a list of important concepts related to a unit of study, then invite students to indicate how familiar they are with each. For example, I might hand out the following terminology list before students read the first part of this chapter:

— Predicting
— Brainstorming
— Schema
— Theory of the world
— Framework
— Prior knowledge
— Idiocentric
— Sociocentric
— Experiences
— Bridge

Students place an asterisk next to terms they know well enough to explain to someone else and a check next to those they've heard of. They circle those that are unfamiliar. A scale ranging from 0 for items that are completely unfamiliar to 4 for items that are understood well enough to explain can also be used.

Like pre-tests, terminology lists provide some information about students' familiarity with certain teacher-selected terms, but tell us little about what else students know about a topic. Unlike the pre-test, this activity doesn't assess the accuracy of students' knowledge. There is a risk that students may indicate familiarity with concepts that they misunderstand as well as those that they comprehend perfectly well.

Helping Students Make Connections

Pre-tests and terminology lists may help teachers find out about what students already know, but they do little to help prepare students for reading about a topic. Other activities, such as brainstorming and predicting, are more useful because they not only provide teachers with information about what students already know but also help students make connections with their own prior knowledge.

These activities have three major outcomes:

— They help students draw on prior knowledge.
— They facilitate the integration of new information into students' current knowledge network.
— They help students set their own purposes for reading.

BRAINSTORMING

We understand new information by relating it to what is already known and stored with the thousands of other items in our network of prior knowledge. Brainstorming is a very effective way not only of finding out what students already know about a topic but also of helping students activate and draw on this prior knowledge.

During a brainstorming session, information that is already known is brought forward and becomes more accessible. If new information is related to this, it can be integrated quickly into an individual's knowledge network. Otherwise, the reader must search through all the items in the network to locate those related to the new information. This search is time-consuming and, sometimes, the appropriate information goes unrecognized. For this reason, encouraging students to bring what they already know about a topic to a conscious level before reading facilitates understanding. After students have brainstormed to bring their prior knowledge about a topic to a conscious level, they read to find out if the items on the list are, in fact, discussed in the text and if the brainstormed information is accurate. In this way, brainstorming sets purposes for reading.

It's important to define purposes for reading. In 1969, Russell Stauffer suggested that purposes "get the reader started, keep him on course, and produce the vigor and potency and push to carry him through to the end." Traditionally, teachers have defined the purposes for students' reading, asking a question—"What is the difference between potential and kinetic energy?"—or issuing an instruction—"Read to find out the differences between potential and kinetic energy."

Proficient readers, however, set their own purposes for reading. Students who don't have the opportunity to do so because the teacher always defines the purpose are unlikely to learn how to develop their own purposes. In an article in *The Reading Teacher*, William Blanton, Karen Wood and Gary Moorman said that purpose-setting in schools is too "teacher directed, perfunctory, and geared to having students locate and recall information." They suggest that inappropriate purposes create problems for students, diverting attention from the major theme to focus on details or divulging too much content, thus killing the desire to read.

Unfortunately, most of the brainstorming models we use are fundamentally controlled by teachers. If students are to learn to set their own purposes for reading, however, they must control this process themselves, with the teacher acting only as facilitator and scribe.

Introducing Brainstorming

Begin by asking students to tell you everything they know about a topic. Out of shyness, uncertainty or fear of making mistakes, some students may be reluctant to participate. They often join in more readily if they are given the opportunity to write several things down on a piece of paper first. When it's time to share their ideas, then, they already have several things in mind. Inviting them to brainstorm in pairs or small groups before sharing with the class also helps reduce the risk.

Sharing ideas with a group or the whole class is important because one student's thoughts trigger others to bring to a conscious level information that may have been buried. For example, when a group of fourth-graders began brainstorming about electricity, they generated a long list. Then one child said, "Atomic energy because it is where electricity comes from." This response prompted a series of others—"What about water power? Don't we get electricity from waterfalls?" "Burning coal, too, I think." "Does a battery have something to do with electricity?"

These children knew a great deal about the generation and storage of electricity that they hadn't considered until one of them mentioned atomic power. Once this was mentioned, it prompted others to draw on information they knew but had not yet activated.

As students suggest information, write it on a chalkboard, overhead transparency, or chart paper. Seeing the items in print helps them keep track of what has been said and allows them to review the information for themselves. Later, during or after reading, the preliminary list can be reconsidered in light of the new information gained.

All suggestions are accepted and added to the list, even if they are erroneous. The intent is to draw on what students know, think they know, have heard somewhere, or have a vague idea about. Misinformation is as important as accurate information because it reveals misunderstandings that may need to be addressed. When students read with this misinformation in mind, they will encounter information that is at odds with the inaccuracies on the brainstormed list. They will pause to reconsider both the brainstormed information and what they are encountering in the text, possibly rereading the text for verification. In many cases, information that disagrees with the original brainstormed ideas is often remembered better than information that confirmed them.

Students' suggestions can be presented in the form of questions — "How is electricity generated?" — and statements — "Atomic power produces electricity" — as well as single concepts — "Generators," "Batteries." To keep the session moving, it's a good idea to keep the writing to a minimum. For example, if a student says, "Atomic power produces electricity," I might write, "Atomic power — elec." Writing complete sentences takes too much time and slows the flow of ideas. In addition, writing in point form provides students with a model for taking notes.

Brainstorming sessions needn't take a long time. Once students understand the process, ten to fifteen minutes is usually sufficient and suggestions will come thick and fast. Be flexible, however. If students are still actively generating information after fifteen minutes, it may be a good idea to extend the session.

Once the initial session is over, invite students to read the passage, then return to the preliminary list. This is the time to add new information, delete or correct misconceptions and identify accurate information so that students can confirm or disconfirm their original ideas and the teacher can see what they are learning. Thinking about the material they read in relation to what they knew beforehand helps students learn the material and provides them with a summary of what they have read.

Once students are used to the process, encourage them to brainstorm in small groups or independently. Because the intent is to provide students with an effective reading strategy that can be used whenever they read, brainstorming as a class should not become a permanent fixture. When it is clear that, as they read, students are relating new information to what they already know, it is no longer necessary to brainstorm as a class.

Evaluating Brainstorming

Considering the ideas, information and questions students offer during brainstorming sessions provides a good sense of what they already know. This allows us to plan instruction that begins with what students know, provides the needed support for dealing with the new information and clears up misconceptions. If students keep their own lists, in groups or independently, these can be used to determine what individuals or groups already know. If students correct and add to their lists as they read, the new information added, misconceptions corrected and previous information confirmed helps us evaluate the content they have learned as well as their understanding of the reading process.

PREDICTING

Like brainstorming, predicting provides readers with a purpose. Once students predict what an author is likely to include in a particular text, for example, they will be motivated to read to see if their predictions are confirmed.

Predicting engages students in a natural part of the reading cycle — predicting, gathering information, and confirming or disconfirming that information — described by Kenneth Goodman in an article in *Journal of the Reading Specialist*.

Predicting also helps develop students' awareness of text organization. As they predict the information texts are likely to contain, then confirm or disconfirm their predictions, they will begin noticing more about the kinds of information that are typical of particular texts. They will also become aware of headings and subheadings and begin using these features to help them organize incoming information.

To make predictions, we use two different kinds of information from our network of prior knowledge. First, we search for information about the topic itself and use this to generate appropriate predictions. If the topic is a country, for example, predictions about location, products, government and major cities may be important, but if the topic is energy, different predictions may be more appropriate.

Second, we use what we know about the text we're reading to guide our predictions. In a social studies text, for example, a discussion of energy will probably include the kinds of materials — wood, gas, coal, water, uranium — used to create energy in a particular country as well as information about why particular energy sources are used. In addition, it might examine the political controversy surrounding the use of certain energy sources or the history of the changes in sources of energy used. In a science text, on the other hand, the same topic is likely to be treated very differently. Forms of energy might mean kinetic and mechanical, as well as solar and atomic. Each form might be defined, along with examples, and described in terms of where it fits in relation to other forms of energy. Our predictions about what we are likely to read about energy in a science text will probably be very different from those we'd make about a social studies text.

Unlike brainstorming, which focuses on what readers already know, predicting focuses on the text. I usually start a predicting session with a question like, "What do you think the author will talk about in this text?" Students' responses may be very specific — "He'll tell us which states were for the South and the North," — or general — "He'll tell us about battles — who won them and where they were fought."

As with brainstorming, the accuracy of predictions is not an issue. In fact, if accuracy is emphasized, students will be reluctant to make predictions for fear that their suggestions will be judged "wrong." During my first visit to a sixth-grade classroom that I observed over the course of a year, the teacher invited students to make predictions. After they read the text, they returned to the list, counted how many were "right" and identified who had made the "correct" predictions.

Not surprisingly, after several weeks of this, the students began generating fewer predictions. Many students simply stopped participating in the activity, while others often read or skimmed the chapter in advance so they could provide accurate suggestions. In neither case were they learning much about the reading process. The entire procedure became a waste of time for both the teacher and the students.

It isn't unusual to find that students predict that texts will contain information that they don't. Sometimes these predictions reveal what students would like to know about the topic while, at others, they highlight serious defects in the text. One class of ten- and eleven-year-olds generated two chalkboards full of predictions about the transcontinental railroad. When the time came to read, however, the text they were using devoted only two pages, including five pictures, to the topic. The entire passage copntained only about 400 words of text. Students were disappointed by the lack of information provided, but the teacher and I used this to our advantage. Because the students were obviously interested in knowing more about the transcontinental railroad, we went to the library and searched for additional information.

Introducing Predicting

While predicting can stand alone as an activity, students are often more comfortable if it follows a brainstorming session because the brainstorming provides plenty of material for making predictions. For example, if someone has mentioned the burning of Atlanta when brainstorming about the American Civil War, predictions related to this often follow — "We'll find out when Atlanta was burned and who did it and why."

Predicting also works well after a passage is skimmed. Invite students to look through the chapter, reading headings, subheadings and captions, and looking at pictures and other graphics. Then ask them to predict what the author is likely to discuss in the chapter. Readers use the textual information — headings, subheadings, captions and graphics — as well as their own knowledge about the topic and text structures to formulate predictions.

These two predicting techniques differ in that the first, predicting after brainstorming, focuses on the reader and the reader's prior knowledge, while the second, predicting after skimming the text, is text-based as well as reader-based. However, they are not mutually exclusive and can be combined effectively. I often begin with a brainstorming session, then invite students to make predictions, and follow this up by asking them to skim the chapter and add to their list or, occasionally, delete unlikely predictions.

It's a good idea to encourage students to keep their own list of predictions even though a class list is posted throughout the unit. This provides them with an easily accessible list to use as they read. They can check off predictions that are confirmed, delete those that are not, and even add new ones as they are generated. Although initial predictions are often made for an entire chapter, encourage students to reconsider their predictions as they begin each new sub-section. These predictions are often more specific than those made for the entire chapter because they focus on a single topic. In addition, the subheading often provides clues for making specific predictions.

After the entire passage is read, reconsider the list of predictions and discuss additions and changes. If students have been reading in pairs or independently, they can form small groups to compare their lists. They will find out what others predicted and why, as well as how these predictions changed. This enables them to compare their own reading process and understanding of the text with that of others, thus confirming their comprehension.

Evaluating Predicting

Like brainstorming, predicting can be evaluated by observing and noting the predictions students make both in a group and as individuals. If they keep individual lists, these can be collected and evaluated based on the initial predictions made, how these changed during reading, and how they were adjusted after reading. Our observations provide information about how well students learned the content, their ability to read the text, and areas of misunderstanding or confusion for individuals or the entire class. This allows us to plan instruction that addresses these areas.

There's nothing new about inviting students to generate their own questions. For years, study skills texts have recommended turning headings and subheadings into questions. Using this technique, the subheading, "Causes of the Civil War," for example, becomes the question, "What are the causes of the Civil War?" When headings are specific, the questions generated tend to be correspondingly specific, while general headings, such as "Battles of the Civil War," tend to generate general questions focusing on who, what, where, when, why and how.

The questioning technique, however, can extend well beyond this useful, but limited, practice of turning headings into questions. Proficient readers don't simply absorb information as they read. They think critically about what they are encountering. They evaluate, react, predict, respond, judge, accept, reject, hypothesize and question as they read. Their questions are often different from those suggested by headings and subheadings. For example, a chapter on the American Civil War might generate questions such as, "What is the relationship between the invention of the cotton gin and slavery?" "Why did so many people die in this war?" "Was it really over human rights — or was it over money?" "Would things be different today if reconstruction had been handled differently? How?" "Was Lincoln as popular then as he seems to be now?" "Did the North really have a united view about slavery or the war?" "Why did the author include this information?" "Who is this person?" "Is he the one who won the battle?" Often questions like these aren't answered in the text being read but lead the reader to a deeper exploration of the topic in other texts.

Introducing Questioning

Because the process of generating these kinds of questions is controlled by individual readers and may occur at different points in the text, this strategy is not a suitable whole-class activity. It often helps to introduce the process after a brainstorming session or by inviting students to develop questions based on headings and subheadings. Asking, "What questions would you like the author to answer?" or "What questions do you think the author might answer?" may help get them started.

Another way of introducing this process—and one I find valuable—is to stop at pre-selected points while reading a passage. To do this, select a passage that is likely to raise questions or evoke strong reactions. For example, a passage that presents the colonization of North America as the hostile invasion of a country already settled by native populations might be used.

Read the passage carefully yourself beforehand, noting the points at which you have questions or comments. With these in mind, select several points at which students will stop reading to record their own thoughts and questions. I usually stop first after reading the title, schedule several more stops at fairly close intervals, then start spacing these points farther apart. Too many stops interrupt reading, while too few limit the thinking required. Stopping points can be indicated by a line, an asterisk or a slash. They need not occur at the ends of paragraphs.

After students read the passage individually, recording their comments and questions at each stopping point, invite them to form groups of three or four to compare their responses. In many cases, they'll find that their comments and questions are similar, but, just as often, they may be quite different. Discussion of these differences—"Why did you ask that question?"—leads group members to become aware of other perspectives on the passage and the reading process. A discussion by the whole class can follow the small-group discussions.

Repeating this technique several times helps students begin to think and question while reading. However, it should not become a permanent feature of every reading session. To help readers become less dependent on the teacher, encourage them to read with a partner, discussing and questioning as they read.

Evaluating Questioning

You can collect the students' questions and comments or simply listen to what is said during small- and large-group discussions. I like to take brief notes about individual students that indicate the kinds of questions or comments they are making. Look for indications that their questions are moving towards a critical examination of the text.

Summary

To help students understand new information, we must determine what they already know so they can build bridges to the new. This involves helping them activate prior knowledge before they read, ask questions before and during reading, make predictions about what they are about to read, and evaluate these predictions in light of what they've learned from reading. Strategies designed to help students take control of their own learning by monitoring their understanding and developing their own metacognitive processes are addressed in the next chapter.

. . . .

FOCUSING ON MEANING

When proficient readers process text, they monitor their own understanding, using a variety of strategies to achieve comprehension. They also involve themselves actively in reading so that the process becomes a dialogue with an author. In both cases, readers think about and respond to the messages they are constructing from the text, processes that heighten understanding, and thus learning.

Helping Students Monitor Understanding

On the first day of a developmental reading class for first-year university students, I gave them a third-grade story to read. The story had been photocopied without the page numbers and, although the students didn't know it, the pages were purposely stapled together and presented out of order. When they finished reading, I asked them if they understood the story. They all replied that they did.

It was only when I asked them to retell the story that one of them finally said that he had encountered some trouble at the top of the second page. When asked to identify the problem, he said that a character in the first sentence on page 2 wasn't mentioned anywhere on page 1. Faced with this anomaly, he had decided that he was just not reading the story right and had continued reading. While a few other students admitted that they, too, had encountered difficulty at this point, most of them hadn't noticed the lack of continuity. They had been able to identify every word and assumed this meant that they had understood.

This incident illustrates a problem common to many students. They neither search for meaning as they read nor monitor their own understanding. Even those who do at least some monitoring often don't know what to do when they're confused. Unable to identify the cause of the problem, they typically blame themselves rather than the text. Furthermore, students often rely on only one or two comprehension strategies so that, when one doesn't work, they either have no alternatives to try or don't perceive that alternatives might be useful.

Reading involves more than simply saying words — either out loud or in our heads. However, the fact is that many students do equate reading with identifying words. They focus on decoding instead of generating meaning, often monitoring their reading only to the extent of determining whether they can pronounce each word they encounter. Additionally, even students who monitor their understanding of fiction don't necessarily do the same thing with infotexts. When reading a story, they search for meaning, stopping and rereading when they don't understand. When reading informational material, on the other hand, they often fail to search for meaning, focusing on word identification instead. Because they seem to expect infotexts to be meaningless, they make little or no attempt to construct meaning from these texts.

This attitude is often the result of training by teachers who unwittingly encourage students to become dependent on them by asking questions to check comprehension and watching for signs, such as puzzled looks, that suggest that they aren't comprehending. In an article in *Journal of Developmental Education*, Claire Weinstein and Brenda Rogers suggest that teachers are often "much more active in the reading process than are students." In addition to monitoring comprehension on students' behalf, teachers also perform other reading tasks for them, such as identifying important information through lectures or worksheets. Practices like these eliminate students' need to read and develop understanding for themselves.

In a report published by the Center for the Study of Reading at the University of Illinois, Linda Baker pointed out that traditional approaches, such as providing study guides and advance organizers, helps students derive specific, teacher-selected information from the text, but do little to help them monitor or develop their own strategies for understanding.

If students are to become active readers, they must be firmly in charge of their own understanding. This means that teachers must refrain from interpreting meaning for them or identifying what is "really" important in a text. Initially, students may not like this. They will seek reassurance, asking the teacher to tell them what is important and if they are "right." If we respond, we will only continue their dependence. We must step back, encouraging them to take control of their own learning by ensuring that they have the tools to do so.

Helping Students Develop Metacognitive Awareness

Thinking, speaking, listening, writing and reading are considered cognitive processes. Metacognition, then, is usually defined as thinking about thinking or thinking about the cognitive processes. We engage in metacognition when we think or talk about our personal reading — what we like to read, what we have trouble reading, what strategies we use when we get stuck. However, in order to discuss our personal reading process, we must first become aware of what it is: we must develop our metacognitive awareness of reading.

We can't improve anything we do — whether it's swimming, golfing, singing or reading — unless we first become aware of what we are, in fact, doing. I can't, for example, improve my golf swing unless I become aware of what I'm doing that's helpful and what I'm doing that's causing my ball to go off in the wrong direction. With a physical activity like golf, I might ask someone else watch me hit a ball and offer suggestions. However, when a cognitive process such as reading is involved, an outsider can't easily observe my thinking. I must become metacognitively aware of my own process; that is, I must learn to observe my own thinking.

In the same way, we must help students monitor their own understanding so they can identify personal reading strategies that are — and are not — successful. Only then can they begin to develop alternative strategies.

Inviting students to mark texts as they read is an effective way of developing metacognitive awareness.

In an article in *The Reading Teacher*, Richard Smith and Velma Dauer suggest developing different codes for different kinds of texts. When reading a science text, for example, they suggest using letters of the alphabet to indicate clear, difficult, important or surprising information. For social studies texts, on the other hand, they recommend developing a code based on whether the reader agrees, disagrees, is bored or confused. Developing the code allows the teacher to direct students' thinking according to the purposes for reading she or he has determined.

Many teachers, however, find it more useful to invite students to develop their own system. Doing so involves them in setting their own purposes for reading, an important element of effective, independent reading.

A question mark, for example, might highlight text that isn't fully understood, an asterisk might indicate an important item, and plus and minus signs might signify agreement or disagreement with an author. Students may also want a symbol to indicate text they think they understand but aren't sure about or that they only partially understand.

It may be a good idea to use only two symbols at first, perhaps a question mark to represent material that isn't understood and an asterisk to represent very important information. Later, invite students to generate additional symbols.

Choose a passage that is likely to cause students some difficulty and ask them to read silently, marking the text as they do so. To help divert their focus from individual words and sentences, try suggesting that they mark anything they either don't understand or think is important. It's up to them to decide what "anything" is.

After students have read and marked the passage, invite them to form small groups to discuss what they marked and why. They are likely to discover that they were not alone in experiencing difficulty at certain points in the text. This can spark a discussion about the cause of the problem and the strategies various people used to solve it. Comparing what they highlighted as important confirms students' choices when others agree and, when they disagree, can spark a lively discussion. In both cases, the content of the text will be thoroughly explored.

Discussions like these help develop students' awareness of their own metacognitive processes. They begin to realize that textual features can create difficulty for readers and to identify the features likely to do so. Because students often blame themselves when they have trouble understanding texts, this provides them with a more positive view of themselves and the reading process. A student who views himself as a poor reader has little motivation to read. On the other hand, a student who views himself as a good reader who sometimes has trouble with certain texts will look for ways of overcoming his problems. When individual students talk about how they resolved a particular difficulty, all the members of the group expand their repertoire of comprehension strategies.

If a whole-class discussion follows the small-group session, groups can share information about the problems they encountered, the strategies they used to solve them and their reasons for defining certain information as important. This helps students become aware of the thinking processes of the entire class. Groups can find out if others had the same problems, whether they solved them in the same way, and if their understanding of the text matches that of others. Because students have already thoroughly considered items in the small groups, they are often more willing to participate in the whole-class discussion. Lively interaction among the groups often occurs. The process also provides the teacher with an opportunity to become aware of difficulties encountered by the entire group as well as specific reading problems that need to be addressed.

METACOGNITIVE JOURNALS

Metacognitive journals are similar to learning logs (discussed in the chapter titled "The Importance of Reflective Writing"), except that students write about their reading rather than about their learning.

Some teachers encourage students to write an entry every time they read something, a practice that can become burdensome. It may be more useful to invite students to focus their entries on a particular kind of reading, such as social studies or science texts, write entries only about specific reading assignments or write a specified number of entries every week. Requiring a specific number of entries every week provides students with an opportunity to write about the reading of their choice.

It's often helpful if students begin keeping journals after they have had some experience using metacognitive marking systems. Metacognitive marking helps them begin to monitor their own understanding and talk about their reading. This, in turn, makes it easier for them to begin writing about their own reading. I try not to specify exactly what students should include in their entries, encouraging them to talk about *how* they read a text rather than what the text is about. At first, they often focus on whether the reading was easy or difficult and what caused the difficulty. Gradually, however, their entries begin to reveal a developing awareness of their own reading strategies and of the text itself.

Here are some examples of entries made by students at various grade levels:

Grade 4

I got stuck on transcontinental railroad. What is it, some kind of train?

Grade 5

The words in the science chapter gave me trouble. I read all the definitions, but that didn't help. I liked the part on solar energy. We have a solar house in our neighborhood.

Grade 7

I can't understand algebra. When we used numbers I could do that. Why do we use letters in math anyway?

High School

Studying for the test was hard in some ways and easy in others. It was hard because there was so much information that I thought was important. There were so many people and dates to know. In the way that it was easy was that the notes really helped and so did the map.

First-Year College

Mapping the tissue chapter was fairly easy. I found that the outline in the chapter could be used as a guideline for doing the map. Everything in the chapter seemed to be pretty much in order and organized, whereas the Jefferson chapter was not.

Once they have made initial entries, my response to what they have written helps them consider more deeply their personal reading process.

It's critical for teachers to respond to students' journal entries. To prevent students from becoming dependent on our responses, however, they should be couched as questions rather than answers, encouraging students to deepen their metacognitive awareness. For example, a comment like, "I couldn't understand this chapter at all. It was boring," might prompt this response: "Were there any sections that you did understand? Where did you first get lost? What do you think made this so boring?" An entry indicating a problem, such as, "I got stuck on the third paragraph. I just couldn't figure it out," might draw this response: "What exactly caused the problem? What did you do when you got stuck? What might you have tried?" And an entry indicating an unsuccessful attempt at solving a problem, such as, "I got stuck on the explanation of mechanical energy. I reread the paragraph, but that didn't help," might spark this comment: "Rereading is a good thing to try, but it didn't work this time. Why do you think it didn't? Is there anything else you might have tried?" None of these responses solves the students' reading problems, nor are they intended to. Rather, they're designed to encourage students to identify the cause of their problems, consider strategies for solving them, and evaluate the effectiveness of these strategies.

It's also important for students to share their entries in small groups, discussing their problems and what they did about them. This helps them become aware that everyone has some problems with texts and that these problems are often similar. They also learn problem-solving strategies from each other. A student who didn't understand a particular paragraph will learn from another's explanation of how she overcame her difficulties with the same passage. Finally, group participation helps students develop problem-solving strategies independent of the teacher.

The teacher, nevertheless, plays an important role in the process, circulating among the groups, listening to discussions to determine areas that need clarification, answering questions, asking questions that provoke further discussion, and so on. When the teacher joins a group, he or she does so not as the expert, but as a guide and facilitator.

The effect of keeping metacognitive journals won't be evident immediately. However, as students write in their journals, discuss their entries with others and consider the teacher's responses, they will become more aware of textual features that create problems and will expand their repertoire of strategies for dealing with these problems.

Journals offer teachers a concrete opportunity to monitor students' growth. We can track students' growing metacognitive awareness and identify the strategies they use when reading. We can also track the growth in their understanding of what they read as they move from talking about vocabulary and sentence length to discussing bias and interpreting the author's meaning.

Encouraging Active Reading

In addition to monitoring their own understanding, proficient readers engage in active dialogue with the authors of texts. To engage actively in a conversation, the listener must respond in some way, if only with a nod to indicate understanding. The dialogue is incomplete if only one person does the talking. When reading, of course, we can't communicate directly with a writer, but this doesn't preclude us from initiating an active dialogue.

We do this in many ways. My own responses to things I read include summarizing important information, commenting on an author's style or mastery of the craft (What a nice way to say that—the explanation is really clear!), noting my own emotional reactions (Great idea! Ugh!), questioning the author (Is this guy nuts? How can she say that?), evaluating the content (This is a poor piece of research), linking information to my own life or work (Could I do this with my students? I need to add this concept to my article), arguing with the author (The problem with this statement is that it doesn't take...into account), and making decisions (Throw this article away). It is unnecessary for the writer to receive my responses.

In the same way, students need to respond actively to writing in infotexts as well as stories. Often, we mistakenly believe that it's legitimate to respond to stories while information in content texts need only be taken in and learned. Nothing could be farther from the truth. Because informational material is written by people with their own built-in biases and purposes, it, too, demands critical consideration and evaluation. To enable tomorrow's adults to be readers who consider critically what they encounter in informational material, such as newspapers, magazines, books, pamphlets and so on, we must help today's students think about the informational material they encounter. A number of instructional techniques can help do this.

DIRECTED READING-THINKING ACTIVITY

The DRTA, developed by Russell Stauffer, has been around for years. It encourages students, as a class or in small groups, to read actively by hypothesizing (predicting), collecting data (reading), and reconsidering their original hypotheses (taking a second look at previous predictions).

Most teachers acknowledge the value of predicting and use this technique frequently when dealing with stories. Far fewer, however, use it when dealing with infotexts, and those who do typically restrict the predicting sessions to titles and major headings.

Making predictions helps us connect our prior knowledge with new information by providing a reader-generated bridge between the old and new. Even when new information doesn't confirm our predictions, it is linked to our prior knowledge through the process of altering or correcting the invalid predictions.

Teachers can certainly provide these bridges for students by, for example, giving them graphic organizers or suggesting purposes for reading. However, these approaches place the teacher in charge of students' reading and foster dependence. A DRTA places students in charge of the process, with the teacher acting as facilitator. DRTAs also help students focus on meaning. Their predictions relate to the meaning of the text to be read, and confirming or disconfirming these predictions depends on understanding the text. In addition to helping students, DRTAs provide teachers with valuable information about students' comprehension that can be used when planning additional instruction.

There are as many variations on the DRTA as there are teachers. In content classes, I prefer to read the text to the students while they listen or follow along in their own copy. This helps eliminate difficulties they may have with things like word identification and encourages them to focus on understanding. It also makes it less likely that they will read beyond the point at which I want them to stop.

To start a DRTA, select a passage that will encourage students to make predictions. A text that combines opinions and facts usually works better than one that contains a straightforward presentation of facts. While it's best if students haven't read the specific text before, the topic or form shouldn't be totally unfamiliar or they won't be able to predict with any accuracy and will quickly become frustrated.

Once the text is selected, read it carefully beforehand to determine the best stopping places for reconsidering previous predictions and making new ones. These points usually occur when new prediction possibilities arise because new information has been presented. They don't always occur at the bottom of a page or end of a paragraph. In fact, I deliberately try to avoid stopping at these places because I don't want students to think they are the only place to stop. The first round of predictions usually comes after reading the title, but can occur even earlier if the topic of the passage is presented.

Read the passage aloud, stopping at each selected point to consider previous predictions and make new ones. Accept and record all the students' predictions for consideration later. I prefer to write them on an overhead transparency or the chalkboard so that students don't become preoccupied with the physical act of writing. Predictions can be marked when they are confirmed and crossed out when new information suggests that they're no longer valid.

I find it helpful to ask students to provide reasons for each decision. For instance, if they suggest eliminating a particular prediction, I ask why. This requires them to present information from the text that invalidates the prediction. Or, if they suggest new predictions, they must present information to back up the new hypotheses. Asking for this evidence keeps students immersed in and thinking about the content. And, as they listen to others' suggestions and consider the rationales behind these suggestions, they become aware of how decisions are made during reading.

As the reading continues, students may become so involved that they interrupt to confirm or disconfirm previous predictions, a good indication that they are reading actively. If these interruptions are discouraged, students may become reluctant to predict or to evaluate predictions except at specified times and the DRTA will take on the characteristics of typical teacher-controlled activities such as worksheets and questioning.

DRTAs encourage students to become active readers engaged in a cycle of making predictions, reading to gather data, confirming or disconfirming previous predictions, and making new predictions. When students interrupt reading to make new predictions or evaluate previous ones, they demonstrate that the goal of the DRTA—active reading—has been achieved. When this point is reached by most students, using DRTAs can be discontinued as a regular classroom activity.

THINK-ALOUDS

Think-alouds are similar to DRTAs in that they involve predicting and responding while reading a text. However, they are different in that there are no predetermined stopping points and all thoughts—not just predictions and confirmations or disconfirmations—are discussed.

In the past, think-alouds have been used primarily as a research tool to study the reading and writing process. Participants were usually given a writing or reading task and asked to think out loud; that is, to say whatever they were thinking as they wrote or read. Their words were recorded on audio or videotape, then analyzed to provide many useful insights into language processing. Think-alouds are, however, also a useful means of helping students become active participants in the reading process.

Select material that students haven't previously read and that is likely to encourage them to make predictions. It's a good idea to use material from the infotexts they are using in class so they understand that this strategy can be applied to the texts they are expected to read.

Although this activity is suitable for small groups, I prefer to pair students. To get them into the reading, encourage them to make predictions based on the title, then take turns reading the text orally. If they read silently, one may get through it much faster than the other. Oral reading also encourages them to cooperate to generate meaning from the text and discuss the reading process. I encourage the pairs to decide how to organize their own reading. They may, for example, decide to take turns reading paragraph-by-paragraph or page-by-page.

During the reading, any thought that comes into the head of either partner is verbalized immediately. When a thought occurs to the reader, she stops reading and shares. When a thought occurs to the listener, he interrupts the reader. The students' initial predictions may get the thinking process going, but their verbalizations may take any form — "Read that again, I didn't understand it." "Is he the guy who ran against Jefferson?" "I don't think that could be mechanical energy." "I saw a solar house once." "Do you know what this word is?" "We were right about kinetic energy!"

Because the two strategies are related, students will find think-alouds easier if they are already familiar with DRTAs. It may also be helpful if the teacher chooses a partner and demonstrates the process before students try it themselves. Make this a real activity, not an act. Use a text that neither of you has read before — newspapers are a useful source of new texts. Reveal your thoughts as you and your partner read together. Students need to see you doing things like questioning, showing confusion and wondering about pronunciations. This helps them dispel the myth that adults never make mistakes or become confused and provides them with a demonstration of the strategies you use when reading.

While students read, move among the pairs, listening to reading, predictions, comments and questions, and occasionally offering the same. This is an opportunity to evaluate students' understanding of content as well as provide specific help to individual students at the moment it is needed.

SAY SOMETHING

This strategy, developed by Jerome Harste and Carolyn Burke, also helps encourage students to read actively.

While I prefer to pair students for this activity, they can also work together in groups of three or four. After reading a designated text segment silently, each group member must say something about what was read. No one can pass: everyone must say something. Once a reader has said something about the text, she can't say anything else until everyone has had a chance to make an initial comment. After everyone has done so, students can then make additional comments, ask questions and discuss the passage thoroughly.

This technique works best if the text segments are short, but not so short that they provide little scope for comment. It's a good idea to select a brief but complete text that presents an opinion on an issue relevant to students. Magazines and newspapers are good sources of articles or editorials about issues like global warming, environmental pollution, school testing or community concerns. Once students are familiar with the strategy, start using material they are reading for your class. Students can work their way through entire chapters, using this strategy to generate discussion.

Identifying Important Information

So far, this chapter has focused on group activities. These are important because they encourage students to begin thinking critically about the texts they're reading and provide them with feedback about their thinking in a low-risk situation. However, much of the reading we do as adults is solitary, involving only an individual reader and a text. Underlining and note-taking are individual activities that not only encourage active reading but also focus the reader on identifying important information.

UNDERLINING

While underlining doesn't require the same level of active reading as note-taking, it's a good starting place for most students because it encourages them to monitor their understanding and evaluate information as they decide what's important enough to be underlined and what isn't.

If your school discourages students from marking in textbooks, plastic or vinyl overlays can be placed over the pages or alternative materials, such as newspapers, magazines and pamphlets can be used.

Some teachers believe that it's a good idea to model underlining by reading from a text reproduced on an overhead transparency, underlining important information, and sharing their reasons for doing so. As an alternative, they may invite students to suggest sentences that should be underlined and why.

I prefer to begin by inviting students to read an article or part of a chapter from an infotext, suggesting that they underline what they believe is important as they read. They then form groups of three to five to compare what they marked and discuss why. At first, they may underline too little or too much but, through group discussions, they will gradually begin to identify the most important information.

Underlining is a useful step towards developing more effective reading and study strategies. It helps students start making decisions about what is important in the texts they read. Comparing their underlining with that of others allows them to verify whether others agree with their decisions.

However, this activity is very text-bound and doesn't necessarily guarantee understanding or learning. Although important information is identified, nothing about this task requires readers to relate the new information to what they currently know. True learning requires understanding and integration of new information into the reader's prior knowledge. Readers make information part of their knowledge system by translating it into their own language — their words.

In an article on study strategies in *Journal of Reading Behavior*, Tom Estes and Richard Herbert referred to certain study strategies as "initiative" because students "do something with the information which might help insure understanding." Examples of initiative strategies are putting things in our own words and relating information to things learned in other places. Underlining doesn't require readers to do anything with the information they have designated as important.

If you have been using activities that encourage active reading, it may be necessary to spend only a short time underlining before moving to something more useful, such as writing notes in the margin.

TAKING NOTES

Taking notes requires more active engagement in reading than underlining. The risk, however, is that some students will simply copy sentences or even entire paragraphs. While they may be identifying important information as they do so, little learning is happening because they aren't doing anything with it. Their verbatim notes are simply memorized for later recitation on tests.

Effective note-taking requires more than copying. To "own" information, readers must put it into their own words. If we can't express what an author has said in our own words, then we probably haven't truly understood what was said. Restating ideas and information in our own words causes us to think about information more deeply. Notes are most worthwhile, then, if they are in the reader's own words.

In addition, notes should be brief. Requiring students to write complete sentences may discourage them from using this strategy because it is too time-consuming.

In addition to summarizing important information, notes can include readers' reactions, questions and evaluations. Note-taking follows naturally from the other metacognitive strategies, particularly metacognitive marking, discussed earlier in this chapter.

Notes can be recorded directly in the book or on separate paper. I prefer students to write their notes in the book. This allows note-taking to become an integral part of other interactions with the text, such as metacognitive marking. For example, in addition to making notes, I underline and use my own personal metacognitive marking system.

If students are not allowed to write in their texts, they might cut strips of paper measured to fit the margins of the texts and attach these to the text pages with paper clips. These can remain in place until they outlive their usefulness. The strips can then be marked to identify pages and chapters and put in a notebook. Another possibility is to take notes on paper. This not only helps students understand their texts, but also prepares them for taking notes during lectures. No matter how or where they're recorded, notes should be brief and in the reader's own words.

If you decide to demonstrate note-taking, match your method to your expectations for the students. If they will be making notes directly in their texts, use an overhead projector and write the notes on a transparency of the text being read. If they will be taking notes on paper, write your notes on chart paper, the chalkboard or a blank transparency. Explain why you are writing each note as well as your choice of wording.

You might also read a passage with students and invite them to identify important items. Once an item is identified, invite several students to suggest alternative wordings for a note and write them all on the chalkboard. This is particularly helpful for students who are having trouble keeping their notes short. After several alternative wordings have been suggested, invite students to select the wording they prefer. This helps them understand that there are many ways to express the same meaning. In this situation, students maintain control over the process while the teacher acts as facilitator and scribe.

Finally, you might place students in small groups or pairs to read a text, decide what information is important and make notes about it. Collaborating with others and sharing responsibility for decisions reduces the risk involved in the situation.

After the small-group sessions, invite the groups to share their notes with the entire class. This provides students with an opportunity to evaluate both the content and the wording of their notes. In addition, this kind of sharing often leads to a whole-class discussion of particular items, which helps students expand their understanding of the material.

At first, the notes produced in this situation may not be as precisely worded as those produced during the teacher's demonstration or with the teacher's guidance. However, students who gradually figure things out for themselves often understand the process better than those who have simply followed the teacher's directions.

It's worth noting that there is considerable disagreement over the value of modeling note-taking — or any other reading strategies — on the grounds that students often fail to practice what they have learned. My own work with students of varying ages indicates that placing them in groups and encouraging them to develop their own note-taking strategies takes longer but engenders a stronger feeling of ownership; that is, they feel it is their strategy rather than someone else's. When this is the case, students are more likely to use this strategy on their own.

Listening to the group discussions and reading the notes created by groups and individuals enables teachers to determine if students understand the text and if particular students need additional help. Your comments and questions about students' notes can help them expand their thinking about a particular topic and deepen their understanding of the reading process. These notes can provide better information than tests or reading comprehension questions because they tell you what the students thought was important.

Cornell Notes Format

This split-page, note-taking format described by Walter Pauk in *How to Study in College* not only engages students in writing important information in their own words but also helps them organize the information.

Divide a paper into two columns, a narrow one about one-third of the way in from the left and one that takes up the remaining two-thirds of the page. The left column is labeled "Concepts" and the right "Details."

Students begin by reading the text, recording information in the Details column. When they have completed their notes, they decide which are related and how. Then, they decide on a label for the concept that expresses the relationships and record it in the Concept column. Students wrote the following notes while reading a passage on the Sahara Desert.

Sahara

Concepts	Details
very big	- largest desert
very dry	- less than 10" rain a year - world's driest desert in ME - no rain for years at a time
geography of desert	- 30% deserts covered with sand - 70% covered with rock, gravel, stones - sand desert called *erg* - ME deserts 1/5 sand - sand dunes on 1/3
temperatures	- day = 120 in shade - air cools fast after sun sets - winter nights = below freezing
transportation	- no RRs across the Sahara - use airplane, truck & jeep - camel caravans still used today

Concept labels shouldn't be too broad. For instance, "desert" could have been used for most of the notes, but such a broad label provides little information about the exact content of the notes. The labels that were actually used are more informative.

Taking notes in this format requires students to think about information in several ways. First, they must identify important information. Then, they must express it in their own words. Finally, they must determine relationships among specific items and generate categories to represent these relationships. Thinking about the information in each of these three ways results in better learning of the material.

Notes taken in this format are also useful in studying. For example, students might cover one of the columns and attempt to recall the information. In addition, they also provide teachers with a valuable means of evaluating students' understanding of information.

Summary

The strategies outlined in this chapter help students begin to take control of their own learning by monitoring their reading, focusing on understanding what they've read, thinking about and evaluating the information encountered, and recording the information. This, however, is just a beginning. Students need to think more deeply about what they read and organize new information in relation to their own prior knowledge.

ORGANIZING INFORMATION –

NEW PERSPECTIVES

Once students have begun to monitor their reading, identify important information and react to what they're reading, they need to begin organizing the information they encounter. Incoming information is not stored haphazardly in our long-term memory: it is linked to items that are already part of our network of prior knowledge. These linkages occur much more efficiently if the incoming information is already organized.

Linking single, unorganized items of information one at a time to the complex of information already in memory can be compared to placing items in a filing cabinet one at a time. To find the appropriate spot for each item, all the files must be searched and it may be necessary to return to the same file many times as items belonging in it are encountered. However, if the incoming information is organized so that all the items belonging in a particular file can be stored at the same time, the process is much more efficient! In addition, the retrieval process is more effective because, rather than bulging with individual items, the file is organized so that the information is stored in related chunks.

Organizing information contributes to the efficiency of the learning process. To organize information, readers must think about what they have read in relation to what they already know. This helps them see connections that might otherwise have gone unnoticed, figure out things they haven't understood, relate information to their own lives, and evaluate the relative importance of various items.

Additionally, the process of organizing information requires readers to view a text from a new perspective. As they look for connections among items of information and determine overall organizational structures, they look at the information in a new light and, in so doing, deepen their understanding.

Charts

Surprisingly, students often find it difficult to create charts, perhaps because they demand an understanding of parallel structures within texts as well as an ability to classify items. However, these "problems" are, in fact, the strengths of charts; that is, creating charts helps students become aware of parallel items, make comparisons and classify information into categories. Charts may be as large or small, as simple or complex, as the material and students' needs dictate. The chart shown here was developed after reading a chapter about human tissues.

Tissues

Types	Location	Function	Texture
Muscle			
Skeletal	attached to bones	contraction	striated
visceral	viscera & digestive	control	smooth
cardiac	walls of heart	movements	striated
Epithelial			
Simple squamous	lines the lungs, blood vessels	diffuse & filter	one layer, flat cells
Simple Columnar	intestines, stomach	secreting mucus, absorption	several layers
Stratified Squamous	lines the mouth, esophagus	protection	single layer, 2 types of cells
Connective	all over the body	connection	varied forms, intercellular subst. of fibers or jellies or both

INTRODUCING CHARTS

Many content reading specialists recommend that teachers provide students with a framework for charts on the grounds that it helps them become aware of comparisons. My own experience as a teacher as well as information gained from interviewing students suggest that this, in fact, causes them to consider each item in isolation. For instance, if the framework for the previously illustrated chart were presented to students, they would tend to treat each section as a worksheet question. What are the types of tissues? Where is each type of tissue located? What is the function of each? They would then search the text for the answers to these specific questions, paying little attention to the relationships delineated by the chart. Filling in a framework requires much less thinking, especially critical thinking, than developing a chart from scratch.

Working from scratch requires students to read the entire text rather than skim to find answers, identify areas of comparison, determine which to include, select an organizational method, and identify headings for categories of information. This requires substantially more thought than simply filling in blanks in a chart.

Furthermore, providing a framework maintains students' dependence on the teacher by giving them clues about the relative importance of information in the text. Rather than identifying what they consider to be important, they rely on the teacher to do it for them.

Students need to understand what charts are and how they help us organize information. Rather than providing them with forms to fill in, you might discuss some charts you have developed yourself for material they have read or work with the class or groups to create charts for particular texts. Once they understand the process, encourage groups to generate charts of their own.

I find it helps to begin by pointing out and discussing the charts that often accompany the material in infotexts such as textbooks, newspapers and magazines. Discussing the benefits of these charts — how they help readers understand the information, how they clarify areas of comparison — helps students better understand both the material and the charts themselves.

Once we've discussed many different charts, I invite students to form groups of three or four to generate one or more charts of their own from material they are reading. While this takes more time than a teacher-guided activity, students usually end up understanding the process better because they've done it themselves. In addition, students often engage in extensive discussions of the material in order to determine what to include on the chart and how. This discussion generates a deeper understanding and better recall of information. While their first charts may not be as "perfect" as those created in a large group with the teacher's guidance, they are far more productive in terms of students' understanding of both the process and the material.

After the small groups have created their charts, I invite them to share their work in large groups or as a class. Each group presents its chart, discussing what was included and why, as well as the reasons for choosing a particular organization. Not all their charts will include the same information, nor will they all contain the same categories arranged the same way. Discussing the choices made by various groups gives students an opportunity to compare and evaluate the information and organizational pattern they selected and to consider alternatives.

SELECTING MATERIAL

Not all material is appropriate for this activity. Entire chapters of textbooks are not usually suitable, although sections of chapters often are. Passages that compare two to four items in several ways are best. Once charts are understood, they can sometimes be developed across several chapters. For example, a biology text in which each chapter deals with an organ of the body, such as the heart, lungs, liver and kidneys, is ideal. On the chart, the organs can be classified by size, location, function, potential diseases, and so on.

EXTENDING CHARTS

Even after students are familiar with this activity, it's useful for them to continue working in pairs or small groups because they benefit from the discussions involved in working with others. However, once they understand the process, they can also create their own charts, coming together to compare them with those of other students.

Charts are also a useful form of note-taking. You might begin by inviting students to make notes on a chapter, then develop a chart for all or part of the material in their notes. Once they're used to creating charts from their own notes, they'll begin to recognize material suitable for presenting on charts and note relationships among items of information as they read. They can then begin to make notes in chart form.

Semantic Maps

Like generating charts, creating semantic maps helps readers organize information and view it from new perspectives. Semantic maps are more flexible than charts, however, because they don't require parallel structures in the text. Webs, in which details branch out like the spokes of a wheel from a major concept, are probably the most familiar form of semantic map. However, it's worth noting that they aren't the only form. All sorts of variations are possible and no single form is ideal.

Many researchers and teachers approach semantic mapping as a text-based activity. This view, which assumes that the nature of the text determines the semantic-map structure that should be used and tries to match particular formats to certain texts, has a number of drawbacks.

First, it focuses on the way information is organized in the text, assuming that texts have clearly delineated, or at least identifiable, structures. In reality, most texts don't. For example, a chapter about plants in a third-grade science text, approximately 1,000 words long, contained several different structures—two sequential descriptions (how food moves from roots to stems and the yearly growth cycle), a comparison (woody-stemmed plants and green-stemmed plants), an examination of cause and effect (the impact of sunlight on plants), and a description (plants seen during a walk in the woods). This chapter is not unusual. Authors don't plan entire chapters around a single structure—they use whatever combination of structures is the most appropriate and efficient way of communicating essential information.

A second difficulty with the text-based view of mapping is that it doesn't encourage students to make connections with what they already know. If these connections aren't made, semantic mapping becomes little more than another mechanical task like outlining, with students identifying each heading as a major concept in the map and the first sentence of each paragraph as a detail.

In my view, semantic maps represent not the text but the reader's understanding of the text. It is a map of the text that the reader has generated in his or her head and may, therefore, include information that is not mentioned in the original text, but is known to or inferred by the reader. The relationships depicted on the map are reader-generated connections, not necessarily those found in the text.

Readers can certainly use the text structure as a guide when organizing information, but should not feel bound by that structure. The major benefit of mapping is that it encourages readers to think about information, including the relationships among items mentioned in the text as well as relationships between information given in the text and their prior knowledge.

This view means that semantic mapping is more than simply an alternative to outlining. An outline reflects the way information is organized in the text. The first item mentioned in the text becomes the first item in the outline and so on. Further, items in outlines can be placed only in one location, which limits their connections to a single major concept. On a semantic map, items can be placed anywhere and connected to more than one major concept or items. For instance, in a history chapter dealing with Thomas Jefferson, Aaron Burr is mentioned early in the chapter in a section about Jefferson's election to the presidency. Much later in the chapter, Burr surfaces again in a section dealing with the Louisiana Purchase. In the following outline of this chapter, Burr appears in two different, unconnected places—under "The Election of 1800" and "Burr Conspiracy."

I. Election of 1800
  A. Tie vote
    1. Two people nominated, one vote, highest person is president
    2. Burr & Jefferson tie in electoral vote
    3. Federalists needed to break tie
  B. Led to amendment that made vote for president and vice-president separate votes

II. Jefferson as president
  A. Foreign policy
    1. Peace, commerce, and friendship with all
    2. No alliances
  B. Domestic policy
    1. Regulate their own pursuits and industry
    2. Encouragement of commerce & agriculture
  C. Democratic simplicity

III. Jefferson as party leader

IV. Budget Problems

V. Jefferson & Napoleon

VI. Louisiana Purchase

VII. Burr Conspiracy
  A. Essex Junta — group of New England Federalists
    1. Fear Louisiana Purchase would bring in new states

2. Old states would lose power
3. Only hope is to secede
4. Needed New York
5. Burr joined the group
6. Hamilton accused Burr of treason
7. Duel between Hamilton & Burr — Hamilton died

8. Conspiracy
  1. Burr visits southwest
  2. Fall, 1806, boat down Ohio
  3. Wilkinson sends message to Jefferson to expect attack on New Orleans
  4. Burr captured and brought to trial
  5. Burr acquitted

On the following semantic map of the same chapter, however, the items related to Burr are connected not only to their respective major concepts—the 1800 election and the Louisiana Purchase—but also to each other.

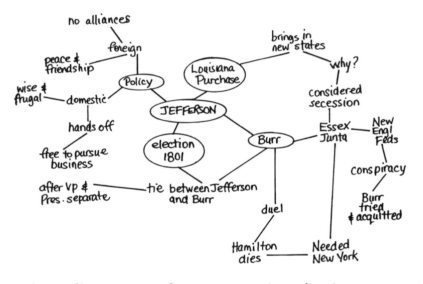

An outline assumes that a text consists of major concepts and supporting details that are related only to each individual concept. In fact, they consist of complexes of interconnected items. They are not one-dimensional, but multi-dimensional. A semantic map can represent this structure more accurately than an outline.

INTRODUCING SEMANTIC MAPPING

Semantic mapping is often viewed as difficult to teach because, too often, teachers have in mind a single map that contains specific information organized in a specific way. Furthermore, many teachers expect students to produce the "correct" semantic map the first time. In other words, they focus on the product rather than the process that goes into producing the map and, for this reason, often try to help students by providing a format for a map.

While semantic maps make useful study tools, the map itself is not nearly as important as the thinking students must do to produce it. In an article in *Journal of Reading Behavior*, Max Peresich, James Meadows and Richard Sinatra present a good example of the kinds of difficulty students can encounter when they are required to produce a semantic map based on a format provided by a teacher. The presidential election of 1920 was the topic in the center of this form. This was surrounded by four concept boxes with three detail boxes branching out from each. The four concepts filled in by one student were Candidates and Issues, Major Political Parties, Results and Unusual Facts. A second student filled in Democratic, Republican, Socialist and Unusual Facts. The first three major concepts identified by the second student appeared as details under Major Political Parties on the map of the first. There is no indication of whether either of these maps was similar to the teacher's.

These two students appeared to be engaged in determining for themselves the important information and relationships among concepts. However, they were hampered in their attempts by the prescribed format, which represented the teacher's perception of the connections among informational items in the passage. Left to their own devices, would they have chosen four major concepts? Did both students identify Unusual Facts because this is a viable major concept or was it the only one they could think of to fill in the fourth blank on the form? These students were required to adjust their understanding to fit a predetermined format, regardless of whether it matched their perception of the information. In some cases, this amounts to trying to fit a square peg into a round hole.

Some teachers believe that students need to begin by filling in a predetermined form because mapping is a complex task that is difficult to understand. However, students understand semantic mapping with no difficulty if it's introduced after they already have experience underlining and taking notes so that they are familiar with identifying important information and condensing it into their own words. The split-page format of the Cornell system described in the previous chapter is particularly helpful because it encourages students to list details and relate these to major concepts. Because their notes are already partially organized, it becomes easy for students to take the next step by creating a semantic map to depict the connections among items.

Semantic mapping can also be introduced by inviting students to write important information on separate index cards or slips of paper. The items should be in their own words and as brief as possible. Suggest that they organize the cards on a table or desk, writing concepts on additional cards or slips of paper as needed. This physical manipulation of the cards seems to help some students begin to organize information. Once they've decided on the arrangement, encourage them to transfer the information to paper.

Finally, students can simply be asked to arrange important information on paper so that the connections among items are clear. I've done this successfully with students from nine-years-old to adults. I suggest that they refer to their notes or underlining or both to supply the information for the map. Because not all information noted or underlined needs to be included on the map, students must decide what to include or eliminate. The only requirement is that they must use a minimum of words and they may not outline; otherwise, the organization is up to them. This technique encourages students to generate semantic maps that work for them.

No matter how semantic mapping is introduced, it's beneficial for students to work in pairs or groups of three or four. This generates much discussion about the topic and the relationships among items, as well as about how best to represent these connections on paper. Even after students are able to create maps independently, it's a good idea to invite them to form groups to compare their maps. This provides feedback about items included on maps and exposes students to alternative ways of organizing information.

Variations on Mapping

Even very young students can create semantic maps. Both the following maps were produced by a five-year-old. On the first, David drew the lines and circles and told his mother what to write in them. On the second, he did some of the writing himself. Both maps demonstrate his ability to organize information. The information on dinosaurs is organized around four major concepts — food, causes of extinction, size and types — while the Starwars map is organized around people, robots, fuzzy creatures, monsters and imperial shuttle. Children are able to organize information at a very young age if the material they are working with is familiar to them. David was intrigued by both these topics and had many books about dinosaurs and space travel.

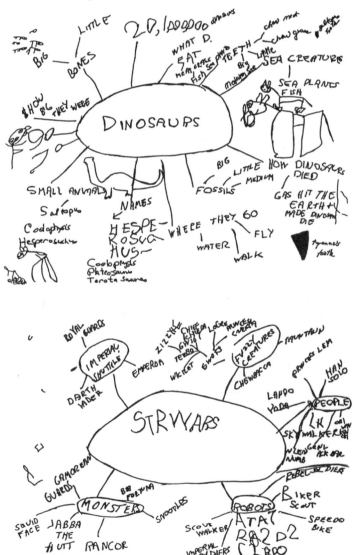

To introduce semantic mapping to young children, you might begin by brainstorming about a topic they've been studying or one related to the time of year, such as Halloween, Christmas or Easter. Write the brainstormed items on cards and invite students to group similar items by moving the cards around. Then suggest that they create a label for each group and tape the cards to a blackboard or tack them to a bulletin board and add connecting lines.

Regardless of the age of the students with whom I'm working, I refrain from producing a semantic map until students are used to doing it on their own. I've found that if I produce a model, the students' maps all end up looking like mine because they assume that it must be the "best."

Because semantic maps represent individual interpretations of a text, they reflect each individual's personal choices. While the information contained on individual maps will certainly be similar, it will not be identical. Some students may include more details because they know little about a topic. Others whose store of previous information about a topic is greater are likely to include less information. The formats for organizing the information will also reflect students' choices.

The following semantic maps were produced by three different students after reading the same chapter about prehistoric people. The first is organized from the top down, closely following the organization of the text. The second is organized from left to right and incorporates a chart organizing information that was comparative in nature. The third places the main concept in the center with other concepts radiating from it. The information included on all three maps is similar, but not identical.

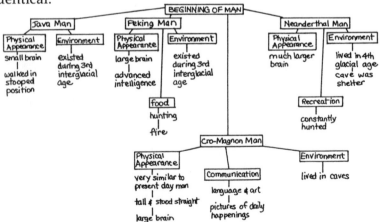

PREHISTORIC MAN	found	brain	posture	characteristics
Java Man	Java Indonesia	small	short & stooped	hunter used fire
Peking Man	China	larger		
Neanderthal	Germany	larger	short	lived in cave hunted animals
Cro-Magnon	France	large	tall	lived in cave hunted animals spoken language artists

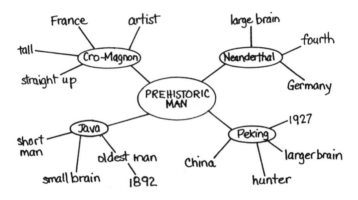

Some students inject graphics into their maps to help remind themselves of the topic, specific information or relationships among the items.

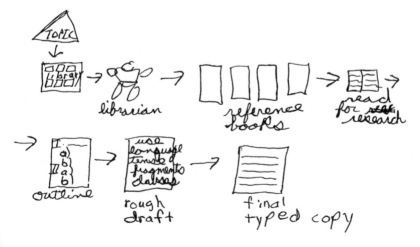

95

The process of creating semantic maps and charts helps students learn and also provides them with useful study tools. In addition, they can help the teacher determine the level of students' understanding of a particular topic. If you choose to grade maps and charts, you must be careful not to base the grade on a preconceived notion of what the ideal map or chart should look like. Simply ask yourself if the student's map or chart indicates understanding of the material. Semantic maps and charts also help us plan instruction by providing evidence that students have understood what they've read or by alerting us to misunderstandings that need clarification.

Summaries

Creating a summary is another technique that helps students learn to distinguish and organize important information. They must determine what information is important enough to include in the summary, then organize it for presentation to others. The focus, again, is on the process of generating the summary, not on the summary itself. Summaries work best if they are written in students' own words.

INTRODUCING SUMMARIES

If students are totally unfamiliar with writing summaries, you might begin with a large-group session. On the other hand, if they have some familiarity with the technique, they can begin by working in pairs or small groups. In either case, students will find summarizing easier to understand if they have already had experience taking notes or creating charts and semantic maps, activities that require them to identify important information and organize it.

A large-group session provides students with an opportunity to create a summary in a supportive, low-risk setting. The teacher's role is to facilitate the process by guiding students through the steps, asking questions and acting as a scribe — writing for the group on the chalkboard, an overhead transparency or chart paper. If genuine discussion is to occur, the students must be in control. This means that they must determine how to organize the summary, the items to be included and the wording of the sentences. To make this possible, the teacher must refrain from offering opinions about any of these things.

Select a passage that contains 150 to 1,000 words depending on the students' age. If the text is too short, there won't be enough information to summarize, but if it's too long, creating the group summary will take so long that students will lose interest. To provide a basis for the summary, invite students to take notes or create a chart or map as they read.

After students have read the passage, ask them to identify the major concepts that should be included in the summary. This process is similar to brainstorming and there may be disagreement over the relative importance of some of the concepts suggested. These discussions should not be cut short because they involve an examination of the content that deepens understanding and learning. The length of the brainstormed list depends on the length of the text as well as the amount of information it includes. The list of items shouldn't be too long — five to ten items is usually appropriate. If the list is too long, invite students to cut it down. This may again generate important discussion as they try to agree on which items to include.

Students might also work in small groups to brainstorm this initial list. Invite each group to identify the three most important items on its list, then bring the groups together to compare and discuss their lists before generating a group list.

It's a good idea to record this list on the chalkboard or chart paper, especially if you plan to write the summary on an overhead transparency, so that it will remain visible throughout the summary-writing process. If the list is on an overhead transparency and you also plan to create the summary on an overhead, it'll be necessary to remove the list from sight at least part of the time — unless you use two projectors.

Once students have agreed on the concepts to include, the next step is to organize them. Invite students to decide whether any of the concepts are related and use a code to indicate these or rewrite the list, grouping related items. Students then decide on the order in which items will be addressed in the summary. If students are familiar with semantic mapping, they may develop a map from the list by grouping similar items, then using numbers to indicate the order in which items will be addressed in the summary.

This process, which involves considerable discussion, helps students organize and gain a deeper understanding of the information. In addition, determining the structure for the summary enables students to see the "big picture," rather than viewing the information as isolated facts.

Once the organization is decided, ask a volunteer to suggest a beginning sentence. Write this sentence on the chalkboard and reread it to verify that you have accurately recorded what was said. Then ask the other students if they accept the sentence. They may suggest changes or completely different sentences, each time explaining why the change is recommended. Add the changes, using editorial marks to indicate additions, deletions, and so on, or write the new sentences. This allows the entire group to consider all the alternatives.

To ensure that the students control the text of the summary, return to the original author of the sentence for a decision about its final wording or invite the group to decide. If there is disagreement, it may be necessary to take a vote. Sometimes, I invite the original author of the sentence to choose the wording for the group summary, but suggest that the students choose the wording they prefer when they write their individual summaries.

Repeat this procedure until the summary is complete. As each sentence is added, read the entire text of the summary to ensure that the sentences fit. If the summary is long, read only the preceding four or five sentences or the section or paragraph in which the sentence appears. When the summary is complete, read it aloud. At this point students may again suggest changes.

During the writing process, students may discuss whether to move to the next item on the outline or if additional information about the current item is needed. They may also revise the outline, changing the order of items or even adding or deleting items.

This process helps students learn. We understand information best when we explain it to others. I've often heard people say that they didn't truly understand something until they taught it to someone else. Writing a summary is a similar experience and generates the same depth of understanding.

This activity also demonstrates the writing process. Sentences are drafted and individual sentences, as well as the entire text, are revised and edited. In addition, the outline may also be revised, demonstrating that organizing a text is a process that is fluid and subject to change at any point. This helps students understand that writers revise freely and often write a series of drafts before deciding on the final text.

A small-group setting provides greater opportunity for each member to participate. Because students are often more comfortable in smaller groups, especially when the teacher isn't present, those who are reluctant to participate in large-group activities may willingly join in when in a small group.

Creating a summary in small groups is similar to the process used with a large group, except that one of the students, who also actively participates in the entire process, acts as the scribe.

It's helpful if the notes, charts and maps used as a basis for the summaries are created by pairs or small groups rather than by individuals because there will then be some agreement about the organization and information selected.

EVALUATING SUMMARIES

Like charts and semantic maps, summaries can provide substantial information about students' learning. This information can be used to plan instruction and evaluate progress. However, we must remember that students' products are based on their own prior knowledge and are therefore unique. Each must be evaluated on its own merits and not compared with other students' maps, charts or summaries.

Summary

All the strategies discussed in this chapter — charting, mapping and summarizing — help readers organize information in ways that make sense to them given their prior knowledge. As they think about what a chart should look like or how a map or summary should be organized and what should be included in each, readers are also helped to view the material in new ways. This kind of thinking provides a deeper understanding of the material. Other strategies, too, enhance comprehension by encouraging readers to consider information and ideas from alternative perspectives. These will be addressed in the next chapter.

. . . .

THE IMPORTANCE

OF REFLECTIVE WRITING

Learning involves more than memorizing and repeating facts. It involves relating information to what is already known, as well as evaluating, questioning, comparing it to other information, responding and reacting. Providing students with strategies for organizing information is one way to help deepen their understanding. Encouraging them to think critically about information is another — and reflective writing provides a useful tool for doing so.

Reflective writing requires readers to view information from new perspectives, a major factor in developing comprehension. Teachers suggest perspectives to students when they invite them to look for particular information, provide graphic organizers, study guides, or worksheets, or ask questions that test understanding or provoke discussion.

Students may also read for their own purposes, thus providing their own perspective. Additionally, their previous experiences and cultural backgrounds may predispose them to view information from a particular perspective or bias.

If readers are placed in a situation that requires them to view the text from a new perspective, they will come to understand it in a new way. For example, readers usually view a story from the perspective of one of the characters, most often the protagonist. If asked to retell the story, they will likely do so from this character's perspective. However, asking them to retell it from the perspective of another character will encourage them to view the events in a different way so that they will come to new understandings.

If you were asked to retell *The Three Little Pigs*, for example, you'd probably do so from the pigs' point of view. But if you were asked to retell it from the wolf's perspective, you'd probably look at the story differently. Your view of events would shift because events that are important to the pigs, such as saying good-bye to Mother, buying material for the houses and building the houses, are not important to the wolf.

Retelling this story from the wolf's point of view requires the storyteller not only to reconsider and reorganize information, but also to present the material in a different form. The three pigs might be depicted as tricky, mean and misleading, whereas the wolf might be presented as starving, sickly and misunderstood as in one version of the story by Jon Sciewitz.

The new forms may include letter-writing, poetry, newspaper articles, journals, etc. Whether dealing with fiction or non-fiction, viewing material from new perspectives and presenting it in different forms requires students to reconsider and reorganize information, leading to deeper understandings.

Journals

LEARNING LOGS

A very simple way to encourage students to begin to write is to invite them to keep journals, sometimes called learning logs, in which they can write whatever they want about a particular subject such as math, science or social studies. Learning logs or journals may contain lists of information, explanations, reactions, questions, application ideas, criticisms, and even comments about an individual's reading process or activities assigned by the teacher.

It's a good idea to encourage students to write in their learning logs for ten to fifteen minutes at least two or three times a week, and preferably every day. Decisions about what and how much to write are up to them. Encourage them to focus on writing what they're thinking rather than on the mechanics of writing — spelling, grammar, punctuation, capitalization, etc. Placing too much emphasis on mechanics will restrict their thinking. For instance, a student who wants to write about the Milky Way after reading a chapter on the solar system may be unsure of how to spell galaxy. If she will be penalized for spelling mistakes, she may choose a different topic so her grade won't be affected. If content is emphasized, however, and there is no penalty for making mechanical errors, she will feel free to write about any topic of interest.

Make sharing entries in small groups a regular feature of this activity. This will lead to discussions about the material, attempts to answer the questions posed in journals, explanations of misunderstandings, and comparisons of differing points of view. During these sessions, students often add new information or ideas to their journals. The small-group sessions should take place at least once a week or for short periods — ten to fifteen minutes — several times a week.

Teachers should also read the entries regularly and respond in writing. While this can be time-consuming if you see a large number of students every day, it's well worthwhile. Students react favorably to teachers' responses to their journals and, in many cases, these responses have sparked them to become active learners. If you can't read and respond to the entries every time students write, try to respond to each student at least once a week.

While responses need not be long — a single sentence is often enough — they work best if they're personal, focusing on the content and avoiding judgments. They tell students that you're paying attention to *what* they are saying because you value their thoughts. Here are some examples:

"I was amazed by the size of the Milky Way Galaxy too. What helped you understand how big it is?"

"You're right, the description of Jefferson in this chapter does make him sound like a slob."

"I don't know the answer to your question. Let's look it up together. Maybe some other kids in the class will want to help us."

Evaluative statements like, "Good question," "I like your poem," or "Nice summary," suggest that the entries are being graded and are likely to inhibit the free expression of thought.

Journals or learning logs are useful tools for informing teachers about students' understanding of material, areas of uncertainty or misunderstanding, and questions about topics. They should not be used to determine grades, with the possible exception of a mark for writing the entries, regardless of the length or content.

Another form of journal-writing involves students in role-playing related to the topic of study. In their roles, the students keep journals, making the daily entries that might have been made by the character they have selected. This requires them to view information from this character's perspective, organizing and presenting it in a new way.

For example, a student may take the role of a pioneer during the westward movement, a fur trapper, a soldier during World War I, a pilgrim on the Mayflower, a native North American meeting the first European settlers, a scientist working on a cure for polio, an oceanographer on a submarine trip across the Atlantic Ocean, or a naturalist studying animal behavior. The character might be a particular famous individual or someone the students have made up.

If students always seem to select particular roles—for example, if the boys always choose male roles and the girls females roles—you might encourage them to select from a list you provide. The list could then contain only roles typically considered male or female. Don't worry if more than one student selects a particular role. This will encourage them to compare their portrayals. On the other hand, selecting a variety of different roles enables them to compare the perspectives of a number of characters on particular events. For instance, ancient Greece might be described in the journals of a wealthy male aristocrat, his wife, a common man or his wife, the children of these people, a slave, a farmer, a soldier, a merchant, or a trader.

This kind of journal entry can provide teachers with information about students' understanding of material covered in class and in texts read. While grades can be generated from this activity, each student's journal should be evaluated independently. Because they involve personal role-playing, they will all be different. Furthermore, if the journals are to truly reflect the students' role-playing, they should not be instructed to cram them with as much information as possible. Chronicling information is not necessarily the main purpose of journal-writing. It's just as important for students to think about how the people whose roles they are playing might have felt and thought. To help them do this, you might read to students — or have them read themselves — entries from actual historical journals.

Letters

Writing letters related to the material under study is another way for students to view information from a new perspective. There are many ways to do this.

If the class is divided into groups, each can be invited to investigate a different aspect of a particular topic. Members of various groups can then write letters to each other, sharing information, comparing their findings, and asking questions. For example, letters between members of groups studying various aspects of energy might compare the kinds of energy, where each is used, the cost of generating each, and other important information.

Letters may also involve role-playing. One teacher divided her class of eleven- and twelve-year-olds into two groups — Athenians and Spartans — when studying ancient Greece. The groups wrote letters to each other, much as they would to pen pals, talking about life in their city. The letter-writing continued for the entire unit and stimulated students' interest in gathering information about their city.

Two other teachers organized a correspondence between their fifth- and sixth-grade students about math. Through their letters, the sixth-graders helped the fifth-graders understand math procedures by sharing their strategies. In the process, they clarified and organized their own knowledge of math. The fifth-graders, on the other hand, had to think about what they already knew and identify their difficulties. In this way, both groups deepened their awareness of math processes.

Letters may also provide students with an opportunity to express their feelings about a topic. For example, they might write to public figures or institutions expressing their views and supporting these with information studied in class. Whether the letters are actually mailed depends on the situation. For instance, when studying forests, a class of nine- and ten-year-olds wrote to government agencies expressing their views on clear-cutting. The same class also mailed letters to national governmental agencies about oil exploration in public wildlife refuges in Alaska. On the other hand, if students write to President Lincoln expressing their views on slavery or to Queen Isabella discussing whether she should fund Columbus's proposed voyage, the letters won't actually be posted.

Letters can be evaluated to determine what students know about a topic and track growth in learning. For example, the math letters written by the eleven- and twelve-year-olds were used to evaluate the growth in their understanding of math processes and the letters about Athens and Sparta were used to determine what students knew about these city states. Like journals, letters can reveal the depth of students' understanding or areas of misunderstanding or confusion that can then be addressed instructionally.

If letters are to be graded, they must be approached differently from other assignments. First, teachers must keep in mind the context in which the letters were written. If students write a single draft, for example, only the content—not the mechanics of the writing—should be graded. Then, teachers must decide whether to consider letters individually or as a group. When dealing with the letters about Athens and Sparta, for example, the teacher considered all the letters produced by each student. In this case, restricting the evaluation to a single letter would have limited the teacher's insight into students' learning. Reviewing all their letters provided a much more complete view.

Additionally, the inclusion of facts may not be the most important aspect of the letter. It may be more important to determine whether the letter-writer captured the feel of the time or the event depicted. In the case of letters written to actual people or agencies, letters might be evaluated according to how well the students state and support their points of view. The real value of these letters may not become evident until students receive a reply.

Poems

Because of the forms in which poetry is organized and the metaphoric nature of poetic language, writing poetry can generate understandings not possible through other activities. Poetry requires writers to condense ideas into as few words as possible, thereby compelling them to focus on the most important messages. This can focus students on issues and feelings and help them capture the essence of a topic of study.

When introducing poetry-writing in content classes, I find it best to provide a form rather than invite students to create a poem completely on their own. In any class, when students are asked to write a poem, they are faced with many decisions: What will I write about? What form will my poem take? What words will I use? What message do I want to convey? Should I use rhyme? Faced with all these decisions, students may be overwhelmed to the point where they become frustrated and give up.

Providing a form supports students' writing by reducing the number of decisions they must make, allowing them to concentrate on decisions about topic and message.

It's worth noting that providing a form doesn't mean setting out a list of rules for writing a particular kind of poem. Doing this will focus their attention on following the rules rather than on the content of their poem. However, helping develop their awareness of various poetic forms through class and group activities will enable them to produce poems on their own using these forms as a guide. Various forms can be introduced by reading examples to the students and writing poems as a group.

Several forms are particularly useful for introducing poetry in content classrooms. It's best to begin with a poem that has a clear, uncomplicated pattern. A patterned book that is actually a poem, such as *Brown Bear, Brown Bear* by Bill Martin Jr., makes an excellent format for young students. Because the rhyme (___, ___, what do you see? I see a ___ looking at me) is embedded in the pattern, the children need not be concerned with finding rhyming words.

Terquains also provide a simple pattern for young children. These simple, three-line poems consist of, first, a single word that is the topic, then two or three words that describe the topic, and, finally, one word that is a feeling about or a synonym for the topic.

Couplets, two-line poems in which the last words of each line rhyme, can be used with young children as well as older students. Two eleven-year-olds produced these poems while working on science units:

I am a heart red and plump
I live in your body and I pump, pump, pump.

To me its such a beautiful sight!
Butterflies so fluttery and bright!

With older students, forms such as cinquains, diamante and even haiku can be used in addition to patterns such as that found in "Beans, Beans, Beans" by Lucia and James Hynds in the Bill Martin Jr. Instant Readers.

Whether youngsters or older students are involved, I don't usually introduce poetry-writing until they are used to brainstorming as a group and have engaged in other kinds of writing in relation to content material. Further, I prefer not to introduce this activity by telling students that we're going to write a poem. Many students have negative feelings about poems and writing poetry. They think that poems are for "sissies," that they are always about nature or romance, and that they are hard to write. To avoid these negative feelings, I simply say that we're going to write something together.

CINQUAINS

Cinquains are five-line, non-rhyming poems with a simple structure. While the rhythm pattern can be complex, involving a specified number of syllables on each line, I use a simpler pattern that's easier for students to follow:

— Line 1: A noun that is the topic of the cinquain.
— Line 2: Two adjectives that describe the topic.
— Line 3: Three "-ing" words related to the topic.
— Line 4: A phrase related to the topic.
— Line 5: A synonym for the topic.

Although the first line is usually a single word, it can be two words that express a single concept, such as Civil War, hot dog, Middle East or patterned poem. The two adjectives in the second line are suggested by the topic and help establish a particular message or theme. The three "doing" words in the third line also relate to the topic and build on the theme. Line four is three- to six-word phrase, not a sentence. This may be the most difficult element for students to understand, but the demonstration usually clarifies what a phrase is. The phrase may describe or portray an action, feeling, desire or reaction.

While the final line is described as a synonym for the topic, this is not completely accurate. For example, a synonym for "car" could be "auto," but line five might also say "transportation," "metal," "clunker" and "expense." Strictly speaking, these words are not synonyms for "car" but, for any individual, they may sum up the idea of a car.

These cinquains were written by sixth graders on topics they were studying in various content classes.

Rainbows
Pretty, Bright
Shining, Showing, Glowing
Pretty Sight
Prism

Sahara
Hot, Dry
Blowing, Expanding, Changing
Mostly Rock
Desert

Division
Hard, Fun
Multiplying, Subtracting, Carrying
Takes a long time
Math

Introducing Cinquains

Cinquains can be introduced as a whole-class activity that involves actually writing a poem. I begin by telling students that they'll need a sheet of paper because we're going to write something together. We begin by brainstorming a list of possible topics related to the material we're studying. For example, if we were studying oceans, topics might include oceans, tides, currents, fish, animals, sharks, whales and dolphins. All the students' suggestions are written on the chalkboard, then discussed to determine which one we'll write about. If the class can't agree, we take a vote.

Once a topic is selected, I tell students to write it in the center of the first line of their sheet of paper. Because we're writing together, I also begin a poem of my own, writing it on an overhead transparency that, for the time-being, I keep on a desk or table. Because I don't want my writing to influence theirs, I don't show students what I've written until the poem is complete.

Next, we brainstorm to come up with adjectives related to the selected topic. With younger students, I simply ask for words that describe it. Again, all the students' suggestions are written on the chalkboard. Students sometimes suggest "-ing" words at this stage. If this happens, I simply begin a list on another section of the chalkboard. This part of the process can take five to ten minutes as students are likely to generate many adjectives. Because too short a list will limit students' choices, I prefer the list to include at least twenty to twenty-five items. Then I suggest that students select two adjectives they like from our list—or two of their own—and write them on the second line of their paper. At the same time, I select adjectives for my own poem.

Brainstorming provides students with a variety of possibilities for their texts, relieving the pressure of generating a poem out of thin air. However, it's also important to provide students with the opportunity to generate their own text, the reason they're provided with the option of using their own adjectives. Brainstorming the list activates students' thinking, but it isn't intended to constrain their writing.

The next step is to brainstorm "-ing" words, including those that may have been suggested earlier. This time, the students select three "-ing" words and write their selections on line three of their paper while I write mine on the transparency. We use the same procedures to brainstorm and select phrases and the final synonym. It may be necessary to explain what acceptable synonyms might include so that students understand how broadly the term is used. I usually provide an example using a familiar object that isn't the topic of our writing.

Once the process is complete, I tell students that they have just written a kind of poem called a cinquain and show them mine. Then I invite them to share their own poems. It's important to spend a substantial amount of time on this. I usually continue until every student who wants to has shared, but I avoid calling on them unless they volunteer. Although all the poems are on the same topic, none is the same. Each has a different message expressed in the students' individual wording choices. During this session, students are likely to comment on how good they are. It's almost possible to see the realization that they are poets — that they can write — dawn on their faces.

At this point, I invite students to choose partners and write another cinquain on a related topic. For example, if our introductory cinquain was on oceans, I might invite the pairs to choose a specific topic related to oceans. The pairs use the poems created during the whole-class activity as a model for their next poem.

I find it helpful to suggest to students that it isn't necessary to compose the lines in any particular order. If they think of a good phrase while working on line two, for example, I encourage them to write it down to use later. Or, they might think of the first and last lines, then develop the poem so that it leads logically from the beginning to the end. During this activity, students often return to their texts to generate ideas, verify information and clarify their understanding. Because developing the poem is not a test, I encourage this as it increases students' understanding of the material.

When students are familiar with cinquains, they can write them in pairs, small groups or independently. I prefer to encourage them to work in pairs or small groups because this promotes discussion of the material we are studying. They talk about the material as they decide on a topic, suggest and select adjectives, "-ing" words, phrases and synonyms, and organize their choices so that a theme is apparent. Whatever the writing situation, find time for the students to share the poems. This gives them an opportunity to view the material through others' eyes, thereby coming to a new understandings.

Cumulative Cinquains

Once students are comfortable writing cinquains, invite them to write a cumulative cinquain, described by Thomas Estes and Joseph Vaughan in *Reading and Learning in the Content Classroom*. Begin by inviting each student to write a cinquain on a general topic such as oceans. Then pair students to share their cinquains and write a new one together. While the new cinquain can incorporate elements of the other two, the students may not use one or the other in its entirety. Two pairs then form a group of four, share their cinquain and write a new one. The groups of four then merge into groups of eight and repeat the procedure. Continue merging, sharing and writing new cinquains until only two groups are left. At this point, the whole class comes together to listen to the last two cinquains and write a final one.

This is a long process and usually occurs over several days. The amount of discussion it generates, however, makes the investment of time well worthwhile. Because the two poems shared are often not about the same specific topic, the groups must make new decisions each time a new cinquain is created. This means that a single student will take part in discussions about many different topics over the course of the activity.

If the poems are displayed in the order they were written, the process involved in generating them becomes obvious. Displaying them also gives students an opportunity to read all the poems, thus perceiving the material from many different perspectives.

PATTERNED POEMS

Before inviting students to use a particular patterned poem as a model for generating their own, make sure they are familiar with it. Read the poem to students—and invite them to read it as a group—many times over a period of several weeks. Once it's familiar, ask the students what they notice about it and record all their observations on the chalkboard. You might start this discussion by asking, "If you were going to write a poem like this, what things would be important to notice?" They may miss some things you consider important but, to allow them to control the process, resist the urge to point these out. This is not a test to see if they can identify everything you can, but rather an activity designed to provide them with a forum for discussing the form of the poem. Things they don't notice during the discussion are likely to become obvious when they actually begin writing.

Pair students to write a poem related to a topic of study using the patterned poem as a model. The following poem, modeled on "Beans, Beans, Beans" by Lucia and James Hynds in the Bill Martin Jr. Instant Readers, was written as part of a unit on the food groups. As with other writing, patterned poems should be shared so that all students can benefit from seeing a variety of perspectives on the material.

Eggs, Eggs, Eggs
Boiled eggs,
Fried eggs,
Big fat runny eggs,
Hard cooked yolk eggs
These are just a few.
Duck eggs,
Hen eggs,
Big fat lizard eggs,
Turtle eggs, too.
Baked eggs,
Scrambled eggs,
Don't forget raw eggs,
Last of all, best of all
I like Easter eggs.

OTHER POEMS

Other poems, too, can be used as models for writing poetry. Haiku and diamante, for example, are forms that often generate different views of subjects and substantial discussion. They can be introduced using the procedures suggested for cinquains or patterned poems or by giving groups samples of each form and asking them to define how they are alike and how they are different.

This session is important because it produces an understanding of the format of each of these forms. For the comparison to be effective, students need several examples of each type. A single example doesn't provide enough material for students to determine the pattern of a particular kind of poem.

EVALUATING POETRY

While the poems themselves can certainly provide an indication of students' knowledge of a topic, the most important information about what they know will become evident during the discussions that take place as part of the writing process. For this reason, it's important to circulate among groups and listen to their conversations. Based on what is learned from listening to these discussions, teachers can plan instruction to accommodate areas of strength and weakness.

If poems are to be graded, it's important to consider whether they demonstrate understanding of the material read. The poems are more than a recitation of facts: they often express students' feelings about topics. A poem about forests, for example, may depict the devastation caused by clear-cutting and toxic pollutants and express concern over the future while a poem about Columbus may picture him as a cruel mercenary rather than a hero. Poems inspire students to reflect and express their feelings about topics of study, indicating growth in their understanding.

Recycled Stories

This strategy takes an "old" text, one that has already been read, and recycles it to create a new one. Recycling stories combines the techniques involved in retelling stories and writing patterned stories.

Like retellings, recycled stories require students to organize information and view it from a new perspective. Writing patterned stories, on the other hand, is a widely used strategy that provides support for students who are reluctant to generate their own stories. They use the structure of an existing story as a model for a new text. The patterned story provides the format while the informational material under study provides the content. For example, using Bill Martin Jr.'s patterned book, *Brown Bear, Brown Bear*, as a model, a seven-year-old child produced the following text about space:

Space shuttle, space shuttle, what do you see?
"I see a Saturn V rocket coming up at me."
Saturn V rocket, Saturn V rocket, what do you see?
"I see a Pioneer satellite coming at me."
Pioneer satellite, Pioneer satellite, what do you see?
"I see a crater-holed moon coming at me."
Crater-holed moon, crater-holed moon, what do you see?
"I see a Land Rover going over me."
Land Rover, Land Rover, what do you see?
"I see radar waves coming at me."
Radar waves, radar waves, what do you see?
"I see a space shuttle coming at me."
Space shuttle, space shuttle, what do you see?
"I see a landing base coming at me."
Landing base, landing base, What to you see?
"I see people overcrowding me."

To produce this story, it was necessary for this boy to think about the objects found in space, how to order them into a logical sequence, and what the overall message should be. His message—I see people overcrowding me—is quite astute for a seven-year-old.

All you need to engage students in writing recycled stories are books with clear structures. Predictable books work best because they have clearly defined patterns that students can recognize and reproduce. Alphabet books and number books also make good models. Although they appear to have a simple structure, recycled alphabet stories usually contain inferences that reveal not only a deep understanding of the material but also students' reactions to the information. The following is an excerpt from an alphabet story written by eleven- and twelve-year-olds studying the American Civil War.

A is for Abraham Lincoln. He was president during the war.
B is for battles which killed many people.
C is for casualties. More Americans were killed in this war than any other.
D is for devastation caused by the fighting, burning, and killing.
E is for escape. Many slaves escaped to the North.

This story reveals that students' understanding of the topic goes beyond memorizing names, dates and events. Producing a recycled story provided the vehicle that encouraged them to think about and express their ideas.

While individuals can certainly be invited to write their own recycled stories, students learn much more when they have an opportunity to discuss their ideas with others. The discussion exposes them to others' views of a text—items considered important and items that should be included in the new text.

The younger the children, the more important it is that they be familiar with the patterned book that provides the form for the new text. I use a text that I have read to them many times. I don't ask them to produce a recycled story until they can read the patterned text with me and we have discussed the pattern.

Older students, aged twelve and up, can be given a patterned book to read and allowed time to identify the pattern just before writing the recycled story.

When introducing this activity, I prefer to write a story with the entire class. We begin by reading the story and discussing the pattern. I usually select a text with a simple pattern because the object is to familiarize students with the process. I also select a text that isn't too long, or it will take too much time to write the story as a group. I tell students that we're going to write a story like the one we've just read and ask them what they noticed about it that we need to keep in mind as we write our story.

Then I tell them that the story is going to be about the topic we've been studying in social studies — or science, math, etc. We spend some time brainstorming to come up with a list of items to include in our new story and write these on the chalkboard.

At this point, I ask a volunteer to suggest a first sentence, although I may provide this sentence when working with young students. This is written on the chalkboard, overhead or chart paper, and then I ask for a second sentence. As each sentence is suggested, I ask the rest of the class if they like it and, if they don't, invite them to suggest another. The class selects the sentence that will appear in the final text.

We continue like this until the text is complete. Sometimes, if we're using a longer text, such as an alphabet book, as a pattern, I stop the group process when I'm confident students thoroughly understand what they're doing and invite groups or pairs to continue on their own.

With older students, it may not be necessary to write a story as a class. I often use a short patterned book to generate a text orally. Once they understand that they will be generating a new text from their content material with a patterned book as a model, they're ready to write.

There are many variations on this activity. The entire class might write recycled stories using the same book as a pattern. In this case, the pattern might be the same, but the texts are likely to be very different. A sharing session provides students with an opportunity to consider the choices various writers made when selecting and presenting the material.

Students might also use a variety of different patterned books as models. The differences in the patterns are likely to spark a variety of different thinking processes. For instance, using an alphabet book encourages students to consider important aspects of events, people, concepts and objects, while a book such as *Brown Bear, Brown Bear* leads them to generate a logical sequence with one thing leading to another. *Someday,* by Charlotte Zolotow, is a book of wishes that will encourage students to think about people and what they might wish for in relation to a topic of study. *My Mom Travels a Lot* by Caroline Feller Bauer presents the good and bad features of a single topic. Every pattern causes students to think about content material in a different way, as illustrated by these excerpts from texts written by eleven- and twelve-year-olds about the American Civil War.

Abraham Lincoln, Abraham Lincoln, what do you see?
I see unhappy slaves looking at me.
Unhappy slaves, unhappy slaves, what do you see?
I see Northern soldiers fighting to rescue me.
Northern soldiers, Northern soldiers, what do you see?
I see my Southern brothers shooting at me.

Slave: Someday I'll be free and no one will sell my children.
Soldier: Someday the fighting will stop, and I'll be able to go home and farm like I used to and not have to watch men die.
Mother: Someday all my sons will come home and take care of the farm and I won't have to do it by myself.

The good thing about it is the slaves were freed.
The bad thing about it is a lot of people died.
The good thing about it is the country didn't split.
The bad thing about it is it created bad feelings between the North and the South.
The good thing about it is the North won.
The bad thing about it is the South was devastated.
The best thing about it is that it is over.

Certain major concepts cropped up repeatedly in these texts and the earlier alphabet story on the Civil War. This isn't surprising as these concepts were stressed both in the students' reading material and in classroom lectures and activities. However, it's also clear that these stories represent more than a simple recitation of information. Writing the stories encouraged the students to think about and express their feelings about the topic.

The patterned books used as models by these students might be considered too childish for this age group. However, I find that there is no problem using them not only with these students, but also with high school and college students. Because the books are not presented as "reading material," students accept them for what they are—books that provide a structure for writing. In fact, I find that many students enjoy reading these so-called "children's" books and will reread them if I leave them in the classroom library.

At first, it may be helpful to use a single patterned book or assign books to groups or pairs of students. Then, new books can be introduced gradually until students have written recycled stories based on several different models. At this point, students can be encouraged to select a book themselves.

In my classes at the university, I introduce this activity early in the semester. I also require students to respond in writing to each chapter of assigned reading. Their responses can be a summary, a semantic map, a cinquain, or anything else they choose. Many of them prefer recycled stories and write them consistently, and everyone produces at least two or three recycled stories each semester.

EVALUATING RECYCLED STORIES

The students' stories disclose as much about their learning as any test I've ever given. The texts they create demonstrate their understanding of the material under study in a way that no form of questioning is likely to reveal. The activity requires students to react and respond to information, and their thinking is revealed in the texts produced. However, because each text is different, recycled stories are not as simple to grade as a test that evaluates the students' responses to the same questions. When writing recycled stories, students themselves choose what to include, and these choices reveal learning. If recycled stories are to be used to produce grades, I approach the evaluation by asking whether the text indicates that the writer has understood the material covered.

The final product is not the only source of information. As students work on their stories, I circulate among them and listen to their conversations. These inform me about what students know and what they aren't yet sure of. They sometimes indicate that I need to provide additional information about particular aspects of a topic or clarify misconceptions. My notes about particular students can be added to a portfolio or used to help determine a grade for the current unit.

Summary

The reflective writing strategies suggested in this chapter were selected because they can be used easily, foster independent reading and thinking, don't make heavy demands on class time, and are controlled by the students rather than the teacher. Some reflective activities, such as dramatizing historical events, are valid and valuable, but require substantial class time and organization.

Rather than outlining chapters or filling in worksheets, the suggested activities engage students in the kinds of thinking that will produce maximum learning. Once they become accustomed to thinking about informational material in this way, they will begin to view it as a normal part of reading. In short, the activities will help them become independent readers and thinkers.

UNDERSTANDING

VOCABULARY

An understanding of vocabulary—the concepts and terms related to topics of study—is integral to all the activities discussed so far in this book. For this reason, vocabulary instruction shouldn't be isolated from the other instruction that takes place in our classrooms. Nevertheless, because it concerns many teachers and readers, it does need to be addressed.

Many teachers believe that vocabulary instruction is necessary so that students will understand what they're reading and learn about the topic being studied. Fearing that students' lack of familiarity with certain terms will interfere with learning, they try to resolve the problem by teaching pronunciation, providing definitions, discussing important terms in class, and assigning worksheets for students to complete during or after reading.

The words worth knowing are selected by the teacher, who also provides the definitions. Rather than asking and seeking answers to questions, students are presented with information to learn and repeat on tests. This ensure that they will continue to be passive receivers of information rather than active learners.

As long as we provide students with information, they have no need to seek it themselves. If we anticipate and take care of the problems they are likely to encounter when reading a text, there is no need for them to develop independent strategies for dealing with their difficulties. Providing students with definitions may meet the short-term goal of ensuring that they pass a test, but it doesn't help them move towards the long-term goal of reading and understanding infotexts independently.

What, then, should we do to help students expand their vocabulary? Should vocabulary be taught formally? If so, when — and how — should it be taught?

Should Vocabulary Be Taught Formally?

Many infotexts highlight new vocabulary by providing lists of words and definitions or, perhaps, showing new terms in italic or boldface type. Consider these words carefully. Rather than simply assuming that they should be examined and reviewed with students before a reading is assigned, ask how they relate to your instructional goals. Are they important? Do they reflect what you want students to know? Is it essential that students know their meaning to achieve the understandings you have set as instructional goals? Are they specific terms that you want students to know?

Clearly, the author believed the terms are important or they wouldn't be highlighted. However, it's worth keeping in mind that the author's instructional goals when writing the text may have been quite different from yours. Or the terms may not have been selected by the author at all but by someone else — a consultant or editor, for example. It's up to you to decide whether the terms are important to your instructional goals.

If they aren't, a knowledge of them may still be necessary if students are to understand the reading. Ask yourself if they will be able to understand the passage without knowing these words. If you decide that a knowledge of the highlighted words is necessary either to meet your instructional goals or for students to understand what they're reading, you must then decide whether they need to be taught formally.

If the text doesn't highlight new vocabulary, some teachers develop their own lists of key terms and concepts. In this case, the same questions apply. If the answer is yes, you must again decide whether to teach the words formally.

A formal vocabulary lesson is the instructional technique most often used to try to overcome students' perceived problems with terminology. But there are drawbacks to this:

— Students cannot learn terms if they don't first understand the concept.

— Vocabulary is learned best in context.
— Teaching words in isolation doesn't provide students with strategies for dealing with problems independently.

The Relationship between Terms and Concepts

A typical method of teaching vocabulary is to provide a list of words and ask students to find the definitions in a dictionary or glossary. This assumes that we learn new terms by simply attaching a definition to them. It is based on the belief that we have in our heads something like a dictionary, full of words and definitions. When we see a word, then, all we need to do is find it in our lexicon. If it's a new word, presumably we simply add it — and its corresponding definition — to our lexicon.

Words are, however, much more than labels for concepts and their meaning goes far beyond a simple definition. My understanding of "dog," for example, includes much more than the dictionary definition. In fact, I'm not sure that I could precisely define "dog," yet I know one when I see it. My concept includes many characteristics that are possible but not always necessary. Most dogs have four legs, but an injured dog could have three. Most dogs have fur, but it varies in length, color, thickness and texture. In addition, my concept includes my experiences with dogs — the time I was frightened by a large dog and the death of my own dog when I was twelve — things I know about the history of dogs, things I know about wild animals related to dogs like dingoes and wolves, and my feeling for dogs in general and my own dog specifically. All this — and much more — makes up my concept of "dog," and all or part of this, not a one-sentence definition, will be evoked whenever I encounter the word. Memorizing a definition, then, is not the same as understanding a concept. Students may indeed memorize terms as needed to pass tests. However, this doesn't mean that they understand the concepts represented by the terms.

When we provide terms for students to define, we assume that an understanding of the concepts will follow. But this isn't how we learn. Think about how very young children learn to talk. How do they learn words? For many years, we

121

thought they learned them through association, the reason we attempt to teach students new vocabulary by encouraging them to associate words and definitions. We thought a child learned the word "water," for example, because we said the word when we gave her a glass of water. This, of course, didn't explain why she didn't associate the word "water" with the glass or cup that held it.

We now know that a child's understanding of a concept, such as water, develops over time. From birth, the child is given water to drink, water is used to wash her face and hands, and she is given baths in a sink or tub of water. Water rains on her house and spurts from a hose used to wash the family car or water the lawn. She sees dishes and clothes washed in water, and water used for cooking.

Throughout these encounters, adults and older children talk to the child about what is happening. During a bath, the child hears about how warm the water is and is encouraged to splash in it. The rain is discussed — "Look at all the water from the rain!" "See the water running down the street." "We have to put on our raincoats so we don't get wet." "Don't step in the puddle or you'll get your feet wet!" The child is asked, "Are you thirsty? Do you want a drink of water?" This language serves two purposes. It builds the child's concept of water by helping her understand what water is and how it's used, and it also exposes her to the term "water." Thus, she becomes familiar with what water is and how it's used by encountering it many times in different contexts. All these encounters contribute to the development of her concept of water.

How does this compare with typical vocabulary instruction in school? When teachers introduce words and discuss definitions or ask students to find definitions, the word or label is often presented before the concept is understood. This means that students are given labels for things that they don't yet understand. The young child, on the other hand, is presented with labels for concepts that are already familiar. If we understand the concept, the label is easy to learn. If we don't understand the concept, however, the label isn't much help.

A parent can't teach a child the word "hot" unless she first understands the concept. When my oldest child was a toddler, I didn't get up one Monday morning and decide it was time to teach her the word "hot." But one day when I was baking bread, she wandered towards the stove with her hands outstretched. I stopped her, held her hand close enough to the stove so that she could feel the heat emanating from the oven door, and said, "Hot! Don't touch! Hot!" in a tone of voice that clearly indicated no. She might not have learned from this one experience, but there were others like reaching for a hot cup of coffee, going too close to the fireplace or too near a radiator. The concept had to be understood before the label "hot" could be used. In this instance, holding her hand near the oven door so that she could feel the heat was one way of helping her understand the concept.

Rather than formally teaching vocabulary in school, it's more effective to help students understand concepts. This means, for example, that instead of teaching the word "photosynthesis," we need to engage students in activities that help them understand the concept of photosynthesis. This might sound like the same thing, but it isn't. Once students understand the concept, they will learn the label easily.

A teacher helped eleven- and twelve-year-old students understand exponents by encouraging them to figure it out for themselves. At the beginning of the math lesson, she asked them to open their texts to the page where exponents were introduced. Several examples of exponents $- 2^2 = 4$, $3^2 = 9$, $2^3 = 8 -$ were given, followed by a page of problems to solve.

The teacher wrote the examples on the chalkboard and circled the exponent. Rather than explaining the term, she suggested that the students choose a partner and try to figure out the meaning of the circled number. She gave them about ten minutes, then asked what they had discovered.

Students reported that they tried adding the numbers to themselves as many times as indicated by the circled number. This worked for the first example $(2 + 2 = 4)$, but not the second $(3 + 3 = 6)$. They then tried adding the two numbers. Again, this worked for the first example $(2 + 2 = 4)$, but not the second $(3 + 2 = 5)$. They also tried multiplying the two numbers. Once more, this worked for the first example $(2 \times 2 = 4)$, but not the second $(3 \times 2 = 6)$ or third $(2 \times 3 = 6)$. Finally, one pair suggested multiplying the number by itself as many times as indicated by the circled number. They tried it and it worked. They had figured out the concept for themselves. At this point, the teacher pointed out the term "exponent" in their text and told the students that they now knew what exponents are.

Rather than assigning the problems in the text at this point, the teacher took the exploration a step farther. She suggested that the students work with their partners to make up their own examples. They wrote the problems they created on the front of a sheet of paper and the answers on the back so that they could later exchange papers and solve each others' examples. During this activity, the students tried things that no teacher would ever have assigned. They were interested in how large a number they could work with and how large an exponent they could figure out. They tried small numbers with small exponents (3^2), large numbers with small exponents (150^2), small numbers with large exponents (2^{20}) and large numbers with large exponents (150^{10}). One pair spent a long time experimenting with zero and discovered that, in their own words, "Zero to any power is still zero!" They had great fun providing the class with outlandish examples of their discovery like zero to the ten-millionth power. Students asked permission to use their daily newspapers, which the teacher often used for math as well as social studies, to find numbers to use as examples.

This teacher then carried students's conceptual understanding even farther by inviting them to brainstorm to come up with a list of occasions when using exponents might be useful. "It's just as easy to say four as two squared or two to the second power, so why would anyone use exponents?" she asked. After discussing this question with their partners, students suggested that it would be useful when talking about very large numbers. They came up with many examples — to say how many drops of water are in the ocean, grains of sand on the beach, and stars in the sky. The last suggestion led them to add that exponents might be used to indicate distances in space because it is so far from one place to another.

This teacher focused on the concept, presenting students with information in an environment that encouraged them to figure out the concept for themselves. She didn't stop when they had reached a surface understanding but made sure they had the time and opportunity to explore the concept for themselves and to connect it to the world outside the classroom. Throughout their explorations and discussions, the word "exponent" — as well as other words that were not on the vocabulary list or in the textbook — was used frequently. Terms such as "two squared," "four to the third power," and "six to the tenth power" exposed students to ways of expressing exponents in words as well as in numbers. In this way, the concept and the terminology were interwoven.

The Importance of Learning Vocabulary in Context

If we return to the example of the young child learning the word "water," it's clear that learning the concept and the word occurred through multiple experiences with water over an extended period. The child learned this word, and many others, within a context in which the word was used naturally. Because water was part of her life, she wanted to understand it, and because it was part of the conversations that surrounded her, she wanted to learn to say it. In other words, it was important to the child to learn both the concept and the word.

In schools, we often expect students to memorize lists of words that they have no interest in learning and for which they see no purpose. While the concepts these words represent may be important to students, the way they are presented usually fails to arouse their interest. They see no connection between the terms and what they know or want to learn because the terms are not presented in a meaningful context. The words may occur in a text students are required to read, but this is not necessarily a meaningful context. If the text is not related to other things in students' lives, it's no more meaningful than a single word.

Children learn many words each day because they are intensely interested. In this situation, the words are easy to learn because they are integral to familiar activities and conversations. A list of ten or twenty words that are unrelated to students' lives is not likely to produce the same kind of learning. Therefore, it's important for students to encounter the concepts and words in meaningful contexts. This can certainly include written texts, but should also include oral texts, pictures and other visuals, and many activities. Terms should be used as part of conversations about a topic and related to the world that students inhabit outside school. In addition, because we learn through multiple exposures to both the concept and the label, the word should be used in meaningful ways over an extended period.

When the concept of exponents was explored in the math class, for example, the teacher and students used the word "exponent" and other related terms over and over as they discussed the topic and shared their discoveries. The final activity—a discussion of when exponents might be used—helped students relate the concept to their own lives. As they continued to work with exponents in the days that followed, this math concept and the related terminology became a natural part of their lives and their conversations.

Helping Students Develop Independent Strategies

Whatever it might accomplish in terms of acquainting students with terminology, formal vocabulary instruction maintains students' dependence on the teacher. We must help students develop strategies for dealing with vocabulary so that they can read pertinent texts independently. This frees up more classroom time for discussion and activities that foster a deeper understanding of the topic.

Vocabulary lists for infotexts, whether they are included in the text or developed by the teacher, are different from those for stories. Words considered difficult to understand may be included in stories regardless of whether they are important to understanding the basic plot. Vocabulary lists for infotexts, on the other hand, are more likely to include terms that are important to the subject matter and only minor attention is paid to other vocabulary that might cause difficulty. Because of this difference in focus, teachers sometimes feel obligated to "teach" the terms on the list, believing that knowing their meaning is crucial if students are to understand the material to be covered.

But, even if we thoroughly "teach" all the subject-related terminology before students read a text, they might still have trouble. This is because they often have difficulty with words other than those identified in the text or by the teacher. Whether they're familiar with the words on the list or not, they may also encounter other words they don't understand. Thus, while vocabulary lists may identify words that are considered important for students to know, they don't necessarily identify other words likely to cause trouble. Because our long-term goal is to help students read texts independently, we must help them develop their own strategies for dealing with new vocabulary.

If students are constantly provided with help, whether it's needed or not, they won't grow into adults who can independently deal with the reading problems they encounter. As teachers, we must help them develop strategies in a supportive environment that includes opportunities to learn and talk about strategies.

Proficient readers use many strategies when dealing with texts. These may include using aids provided in the text, using context clues, reading on, and consulting another source.

USING TEXTUAL AIDS

Texts often provide a variety of aids for readers. For example, important words are often listed at the beginning or end of chapters to alert readers to terms they need to understand and learn, italic or boldface type is sometimes used to highlight important words in the body of the text, many textbooks include a glossary of important terms, and, in some texts, definitions are found in the margins. In addition, many infotexts also provide pronunciation guides.

Students need to be aware of the ways their texts can help them with vocabulary. This can often be accomplished by simply pointing out the particular aids. Teachers must realize, however, that even when all these aids are used, students can still have trouble for a variety of reasons.

First, the definitions provided in the glossary or margins are often unclear or too brief to provide a thorough understanding of the concept. In general, they include only a one-sentence definition, providing little explanation and no examples that might clarify the term. Defining kinetic energy as energy of motion, for example, is too brief to provide a clear understanding of the term. In addition, this definition, like many others, defines the word by using another difficult term. If students don't know what energy or energy of motion mean, they won't understand either term.

Second, words defined in the margin or glossary are not always those that create difficulty for students. For example, the highlighted word in a paragraph in one biology text is "ontogeny." However, students also had trouble with other words in the same passage, such as "vertebrate," "embryo," "embryonic stages," "amphibian," "recapitulation" and "elaborated."

Thus, although many texts provide help for readers, the aids are not always useful.

USING CONTEXT CLUES

Using context clues—examining how a word is used to figure out its meaning—is a strategy that is frequently used by proficient readers. Context clues are often—but not always—embedded in the sentence that contains the difficult word. Students need to know that reading the preceding and following sentence, or sentences, may also provide information about a word's meaning. This information may include a definition, an example, or an explanation.

For example, a definition of the word "tariff" follows the first appearance of the word in *The United States and Other Americas*:

> The first quarrel was about tariff. A tariff is a tax paid on goods brought into a country from foreign countries.

Examples of energy are provided in the sentences that follow the introduction of the word in this passage from *Accent on Science*:

> Objects that are not in motion can also have energy. A car stopped at the top of a hill has energy. This type of energy is called potential (puh TEN chul) energy. Potential energy is energy that is stored. For example, the stopped car has potential energy because of its position on the top of the hill. Another example of potential energy is a stretched rubber band. Because of its stretched position, it has potential energy. If you let go of the stretched rubber band, it will move.

In the following passage from *Silver Burdett Science*, the term "frost action" is preceded by an explanation of what it is:

> In some mountain regions, the daytime temperatures are above the freezing point of water. Water seeps into

cracks in rock. At night, temperatures drop below the freezing point. So the water turns to ice. When water freezes, it expands. As the water in a crack expands, it pushes with great force against both sides of the crack. This causes the crack to become larger. The daily freezing and melting of water causes large rocks to break up into smaller pieces. This kind of physical weathering is called frost action.

Context clues are not always as obvious as in the preceding examples. In the following passage from *Exploring Our World: The Americas*, the term "migrating" is not defined, but readers can figure out what it means by reading the following text, which describes the migration that took place:

> From colonial times, Americans had been migrating westward from the Atlantic Coast to settle western lands. Settlers had crossed the western plains and the mountains to settle in the Pacific Coast region. But they had bypassed the vast semiarid parts of the Interior Plains and only a few people had moved into the Rocky Mountain region. After the war, Americans began moving into these remaining unsettled parts of our nation. Thousands of young people went west to the Rockies to work in the newly opened gold and silver mines. Railroads were built across the continent, tying East and West together. Many more people moved west then.

Like aids embedded in the text, however, context clues are not always available or helpful. Definitions included in the body of a text are often as troublesome as those highlighted in the margins or glossary — they're too brief to be helpful or include other difficult words. Regrettably, infotexts that provide useful examples and clear explanations are the exception, not the rule. In the following passage about ribosomes from *Textbook of Anatomy and Physiology*, additional information is provided, but it contains many specialized terms that were only recently introduced. If students haven't had time to absorb these concepts — light microscope, electron microscope, endoplasmic reticulum, cytoplasm — they are likely to become hopelessly lost when reading this paragraph:

> Ribosomes are small structures composed of ribonucleic acid and protein. Although they are too small to be

seen with a light microscope, the electron microscope reveals hundreds of these little spheres. Many are attached to the endoplasmic reticulum, but many others are scattered through the cytoplasm.

Context clues can also fail to provide essential information about key terms. Students reading the following description of the underground railroad from a chapter on the American Civil War in *The United States and Other Americas* thought it was some kind of a subway. They combined their knowledge "underground" (beneath the ground), "railroad" and "stations" with their understanding that this was a form of transportation to reach this conclusion. Nothing in the text disconfirms their reasoning. In this case, the explanation in the text actually contributed to the misunderstanding.

An underground railroad is a means of helping slaves escape to freedom. Hiding places, or "stations," were provided along routes for runaway slaves. The slaves were fed and taken from one point to another until they reached Canada.

Using context clues becomes more difficult when new concepts are introduced too quickly. Readers don't have time to fully understand one new concept before a second is encountered. In one ten-page chapter in a science book, eight major forms of energy are introduced, each with several sub-types. The first page of this chapter is a full-page picture and illustrations occupy at least half the space on the remaining pages. The text itself is approximately 1,000 words long. If this is averaged, it works out to about 125 words per concept. In this chapter, however, the author allocates a little more than 200 words to the uses of radio signals and radar, while defining radiant energy in two sentences totalling twenty-two words — "Radiant energy is a form of energy that travels in waves. Radiant energy can be transferred between objects separated by empty space." While radio signals and radar are forms of radiant energy, they appear in separate sections of the text and their connection to radiant energy isn't explained. Students reading the chapter, then, view them as separate topics.

There is a further problem with this particular text — the definitions provided build on each other. This means that if readers don't understand one term, they have little hope of understanding what follows. Readers of this chapter encounter many new concepts, all of which are important, within a very brief section of text that provides little support for understanding.

READING ON

Because many context clues occur after unfamiliar terms are first encountered, an important strategy used by proficient readers is to continue reading. They know that information that clarifies the problem term may show up in the next few sentences, the next paragraph, or even several pages later. They also know that it isn't necessary to identify the meaning of every word in order to understand the topic. In the passage about the westward movement cited in the previous section, it isn't absolutely necessary for students to grasp the meaning of "migrating" as long as they know that people were moving west.

In several of his books, Frank Smith recommends that readers keep reading when they encounter difficulty with a text. He points out that continuing the flow of thought is a major factor that contributes to comprehension. When the flow is interrupted to figure out the meaning of a word, readers lose their train of thought and have trouble relating subsequent information to ideas encountered before the difficulty cropped up. Rather than stopping to decode a particular word, he suggests that readers keep going and return to the problem spots later or even read the entire chapter again. During a second reading, things that were confusing often become clear because the reader's prior knowledge is expanded.

Comprehension occurs when readers are able to relate what they are encountering to their own prior knowledge. Completing the reading allows at least some information about a topic to be related to readers' network of prior knowledge. These new connections contribute to readers' comprehension during a second reading.

Some teachers hesitate to suggest that students read on, fearing that doing so only encourages them to skip or ignore important information. The advantages, however, outweigh the disadvantages. Reading on keeps students from getting stuck in one place and provides them with additional information that can be used to understand a problem word or passage. Students often believe that they must identify every word they encounter. If they can't figure out a word, they often read no farther, believing that not knowing the word will keep them from understanding the rest of the text. They could, of course, stop and look up the word in the glossary or a dictionary, but this creates a major interruption in the flow of reading.

CONSULTING ANOTHER SOURCE

If textual aids and context clues don't help clear up misunderstandings and reading on or rereading haven't worked, readers can consult another source. This source might be a person or another text. If one text defines a term inadequately, a second may clearly explain the concept and provide examples as well. Dictionaries may provide definitions of terms, but they often don't include definitions that are specific to the subject matter being studied. Terms specific to particular subject areas are often not even included in dictionaries. In addition, dictionary definitions are usually very brief. They may define the word, but they don't explain the concept.

The World Book Dictionary defines "ribosome" as a small structure in the cytoplasm of cells that carries on protein synthesis. This definition is no more helpful than the text definition discussed earlier. In fact, it is incomprehensible unless you know what cells, the cytoplasm of cells and protein synthesis are.

Helping Students Deal with Unfamiliar Vocabulary

The strategies outlined in the previous section can be pointed out to students, but—as every teacher knows—this advice is often heard but not applied. Exercises that require students to use context clues or refer to dictionaries are frequently viewed as nothing more than another assignment that bears no relation to reading.

To help students deal with unfamiliar vocabulary, teachers must provide opportunities for them to understand the concepts they are likely to encounter and develop strategies for dealing independently with reading difficulties.

Most difficulties with vocabulary arise not because students can't identify the words but because they are unfamiliar with the concepts. Often, students have trouble relating what they already know to the new concepts they encounter. Teachers can help overcome this by providing information about topics of study in a variety of forms and by engaging students in activities that help them understand various related concepts. Because we learn by relating new information to what is already known, it makes sense to start with what students already know. This means that we must first determine what they know about the topic in question.

Even when a topic seems remote from their lives and the formal terminology is unfamiliar, students often have some understanding of the concept. When one teacher, for example, asked a class of ten- and eleven-year-old students to tell him about the phases of the moon, they looked at him with blank faces. But when he asked them to tell him what they had noticed about the way the moon looks on different nights, they told him a lot.

Students might not be able to explain a concept in formal terms, but they often possess understandings that help them make connections to topics of study. A study of photosynthesis, for example, might be introduced by asking students what they know about how plants grow. Their ideas about sunlight, water and the parts of a plant can form the basis for study. Diagrams of plants, films of plant growth, experiments with plants, and reading a variety of texts can all lead to an understanding of the concept.

A good way to find out what students know is to start with a brainstorming session about the topic. This provides the teacher with information about what students already know, as well as their misperceptions. The brainstormed list can be used as a basis for discussing information students gain from their reading and may suggest some basic conceptual understandings that may need to be addressed before they begin reading. Explaining concepts is not enough: the texts do this. Teachers must use other means to help students understand, such as videotapes, films, filmstrips, experiments, demonstrations and activities.

For example, if the texts don't provide a clear definition or example of energy and students don't understand the concept, it's a good idea to plan activities, experiments, demonstrations, or a film to help them understand what energy is before they begin reading a chapter about the kinds of energy. The math teacher who provided examples of exponents and invited students to figure them out was, in a sense, engaging them in an experiment. Students studied data (the examples), generated hypotheses (their explanations), and tested their hypotheses (by comparing their answers with those for the examples). Their experiments — and the subsequent discussions — helped them understand exponents.

DEVELOPING STRATEGIES

In her book, *Lessons from a Child*, Lucy McCormick Calkins says that teachers who provide students with topics for writing and tell them how to spell words promote dependence. She calls this dependence on the teacher "writers' welfare." In the same way, identifying vocabulary for students, then providing them with definitions of those words promotes "readers' welfare." Rather than promoting this dependence, we need to encourage independent reading. In addition to being responsible for their reading, students need to have opportunities to confirm their decisions and understandings and learn new strategies for dealing with problems. These goals can be achieved through individual and small- and large-group activities and discussions, a process that encourages students to think and talk about not only the content of their reading but also the reading process itself. Activities that promote independent reading while stressing vocabulary are predicting meaning, using trouble slips and identifying important concepts.

Predicting Meaning

Predicting is a useful way to help students take charge of their own reading and focus on meaning as they read. Techniques for predicting what a text will be about were discussed earlier. A similar technique can be used with vocabulary.

Begin with a list of terms students are likely to encounter in their reading and invite them to tell what they think each word means. Present the words in isolation — don't use them in a sentence or read the paragraph in which the word is found. In some cases, students may actually know the words, but, if not, encourage them to predict what they mean.

I usually ask students to write their predicted definitions individually, then I place them in groups to discuss their predictions. This discussion often helps them become aware of features of the words themselves. One student, for example, suggested that "compromise" had something to do with "promise" because it includes that word. Another suggested that an "abolitionist" is a person because it ends like "communist" and "psychologist." Observations like these help students remember particular words and develop their awareness of connections among words and spellings that relate to meaning.

After small groups of students discuss their predictions, these can be shared with the entire class before the text is read. Or students can read the text immediately after the small-group discussion. After the reading, students look over their predictions individually and change or add to them as necessary. This gives them an opportunity to confirm or revise their own personal predictions. Then they return to their small groups to discuss the new definitions. This provides additional confirmation as they discover whether other definitions match theirs. Finally, the entire class discusses the words and what they mean.

While this activity is certainly useful, if used too frequently, it can become just another assignment. Its major drawback is that it's controlled by the teacher — who makes up the original word list — rather than the students. This means that words the students think are important or difficult might not be discussed at all.

Using Trouble Slips

Rather than giving students ready-made vocabulary lists, it's a good idea to ask them to read a passage and identify words they don't clearly understand. I suggest that they write the troublesome words on slips of paper resembling bookmarks, place these in the book to mark the page where the difficulty occurred, and continue reading. This technique places responsibility for understanding squarely with the reader and conveys the message that students should be reading to understand. Trouble slips also suggest that they should read on when they encounter difficulty, while providing them with a way of keeping track of what they need to reread.

When they finish reading, students return to the places they've marked. If they now understand, they throw away the trouble slip; if they're still confused, they leave it where it is. Then they form groups to discuss all the places that have been marked. Sometimes, only one student has marked a particular spot while, at other times, several students find that they had difficulty in the same place. In either case, all the students work together to achieve understanding. Portions of the text that continue to cause trouble are brought to a whole-class discussion. Through the small- and large-group discussions, students confirm their understandings, clarify misunderstandings, and learn strategies for figuring out words.

An important advantage of this strategy is that it is student-controlled. Students have an opportunity to identify all the things that give them difficulty — and are not restricted to examining only those items identified in the text. This ensures that all difficult vocabulary is discussed.

Using trouble slips is related to the metacognitive strategies discussed earlier. Like keeping journals and metacognitive marking, in which students mark important ideas or things they don't understand in their texts, using trouble slips expands reading strategies and promotes metacognitive awareness and independent reading. In all three cases, the items identified as problematic may be words, phrases, sentences or even paragraphs.

Identifying Important Concepts

When students read, I sometimes ask them to identify important concepts and record important information about each. Because I want them to focus on the concepts, this involves more than simply writing a list of words. Their notes may include definitions, examples and explanations, as well as delineate relationships with other concepts. Like using trouble slips, this activity places responsibility for reading and understanding with the students. They decide what is important and why.

Once students have independently identified important concepts, they meet in small groups to compare their lists and develop a group list. Finally, the whole class meets to compare and discuss the concepts. As students present their concepts, they explain why they think they are important and others have an opportunity to question their decisions or speak in favor of them by adding supportive information.

While teachers sometimes worry that students won't identify all the important concepts, I have yet to encounter a situation where this happened. Although a single individual might not include the same concepts as the teacher, this is taken care of in the small- and large-group sessions when the students discuss their lists. I usually find that they identify much more than the teacher.

It's worth noting that students are also identifying important concepts when they underline important ideas in their text and write notes and engage in charting, semantic mapping and writing summaries, techniques that were discussed earlier. In these cases, identifying important concepts is integral to the activities, rather than a separate activity.

Summary

Teachers can do many things to help students understand concepts and develop strategies for dealing with vocabulary. However, these activities should not be carried out in isolation. The activities discussed in this chapter are simply extensions of other activities discussed earlier in the book. When students predict, use metacognitive marking, take notes, write summaries, make semantic maps, and write reflectively, they are thinking and talking about the concepts they need to learn and using the appropriate terminology to do so. It is through opportunities to think, talk and write about the topic that they come to understand both the concepts and the labels.

. . . .

BIBLIOGRAPHY

Professional References

Adams, M. *Beginning to Read: Thinking and Learning about Print.* Cambridge, Massachusetts: The MIT Press, 1990.

Baker, L. *Do I Understand or Do I Not Understand: That Is the Question.* Reading Education Report No.10. Urbana, Illinois: University of Illinois, Center for the Study of Reading, 1979.

Barnes, D. *From Communication to Curriculum.* New York: Penguin, 1975.

Baumann, J. & J. Serra. "The Frequency and Placement of Main Ideas in Children's Social Studies Textbooks: A Modified Replication of Braddock's Research on Topic Sentences." In *Journal of Reading Behavior.* Vol. 16, No. 1 (1984).

Bernstein, H. "When More Is Less: The Mentioning Problem in Textbooks." In *American Educator.* Vol. 9, No. 2 (1985).

Blanton, W., K. Wood & G. Moorman. "The Role of Purpose in Reading Instruction." In *The Reading Teacher.* Vol. 34, No. 6 (1990).

Britton, J., T. Burgess, N. Martin, A. McLeod & H. Rosen. *The Development of Writing Abilities.* London: Macmillan, 1975.

Bruner, J. *Actual Minds, Possible Worlds.* Cambridge, Massachusetts: Harvard University Press, 1986.

Calkins, L. *Lessons from a Child.* Portsmouth, New Hampshire: Heinemann, 1983.

Canney, G. & Winograd, P. *Schemata for Reading and Reading Comprehension Performance.* Technical Report No. 120. Urbana, Illinois: University of Illinois, Center for the Study of Reading, 1979.

Clay, M. *Reading: The Patterning of Complex Behavior.* Auckland, New Zealand: Heinemann, 1973.

Dansereau, D. *Learning Strategies.* New York: Academic Press, 1978.

Dansereau, D., G. Long, B. McDonald & T. Atkinson. *Learning Strategy Inventory and Development and Assessment.* Lowry Air Force Base, Colorado: Air Force Human Resources Laboratory, 1975.

Duffy, G. & L. Roehler. "Teaching Reading Skills as Strategies." In *The Reading Teacher.* Vol. 40, No. 4 (1987).

Estes, T. & R. Herbert. "Habits of Study and Test Performance." *Journal of Reading Behavior.* Vol. 17, No. 1 (1985).

Estes, T. & J. Vaughan. *Reading and Learning in the Content Classroom.* 2nd. Ed. Boston, Massachusetts: Allyn & Bacon, 1985.

Farr, R. & R. Carey. *Reading: What Can Be Measured?* 2nd Ed. Newark, Delaware: International Reading Association, 1986.

Feathers, K. & F. Smith. "Meeting the Reading Demands of the Real World: Literacy-Based Content Instruction." In *Journal of Reading.* Vol. 30, No. 6 (1987).

Flower, L. & J.R. Hayes. "A Cognitive Process Theory of Writing. In *College Composition and Communication.* Vol. 32, No. 4 (1981).

Garner, R. & N. Taylor. "Monitoring of Understanding: An Investigation of Attentional Assistance Needs at Different Grade and Reading Proficiency Levels. In *Reading Psychology.* Vol. 3, No. 1 (1982).

Goodman, K. "A Psycholinguistic Guessing Game." In *Journal of the Reading Specialist.* Vol. 6, No. 4 (1967).

Graves, D. *A Researcher Learns to Write.* Exeter, New Hampshire: Heinemann, 1984.

Hare, V.C. & D.C. Smith. "Reading to Remember: Studies of Metacognitive Reading Skills in Elementary School-Aged Children." In *Journal of Educational Research*. Vol. 15, No. 3 (1982).

Harms, J. & L. Lettow. "Fostering Ownership of the Reading Experience." In *The Reading Teacher*. Vol. 40, No. 3 (1986).

Harste, J. *New Policy Guidelines in Reading: Connecting Research and Practice*. Urbana, Illinois: National Council of Teachers of English, 1989.

Harste, J. & R. Carey. "Comprehension as Setting." In *New Perspectives on Comprehension*. Bloomington, Indiana: Indiana University Press, 1979.

Harste, J., K. Short & C. Burke. *Creating Classrooms for Authors*. Portsmouth, New Hampshire: Heinemann, 1988.

Harste, J., V. Woodward & C. Burke. *Language Stories and Literacy Lessons*. Portsmouth, New Hampshire: Heinemann, 1984.

Hidi, S. & A. Hildyard. "The Comparison of Oral and Written Productions in Two Discourse Modes." In *Discourse Processes*. Vol. 6, No. 2 (1983).

Holdaway, D. *The Foundations of Literacy*. Gosford, New South Wales: Ashton Scholastic, 1979.

Irwin, J. & C. Davis. "Assessing Readability: The Checklist Approach." In *Journal of Reading*. Vol. 24, No. 2 (1980).

Johns, J. & D. Ellis. "Reading: Children Tell It like It Is." In *Reading World*. Vol. 16, No. 2 (1976).

Kent. C. "A Linguist Compares Narrative and Expository Prose." In *Journal of Reading*. Vol. 28, No. 3 (1984).

Langer, J. "Children's Sense of Genre: A Study of Performance on Parallel Reading and Writing." In *Written Communication*. Vol. 2, No. 2 (1985).

Meyers, J. *Writing to Learn across the Curriculum*. Bloomington, Indiana: Phi Delta Kappa Educational Foundation, 1984.

Miccinati, J.L. "Mapping the Terrain: Connecting Reading with Academic Writing." In *Journal of Reading*. Vol. 31, No. 6 (1988).

Moffett, J. *Teaching the Universe of Discourse*. Boston, Massachusetts: Houghton Mifflin, 1968.

Nahrgang, C. & B. Petersen. "Using Writing to Learn Mathematics." In *Mathematics Teacher*. Vol. 7, No. 6 (1986).

Nejad-Asghar, I. *The Schema: A Structural or a Functional Pattern?* Technical Report No. 159. Urbana, Illinois: University of Illinois, Center for the Study of Reading, 1980.

Nist, S.L. & M.L. Simpson. "PLAE, A Validated Study Strategy." In *Journal of Reading*. Vol. 33, No. 3 (1989).

Pappas, C., B. Kiefer & L. Levstik. *An Integrated Language Perspective in the Elementary School: Theory into Action*. White Plains, New York: Longman, 1990.

Pappas, C. "Fostering Full Access to Literacy by Including Information Books." In *Language Arts*. Vol. 68, No. 6 (1991).

Pauk, W. *How to Study in College*. 3rd Ed. Boston, Massachusetts: Houghton Mifflin, 1984.

Pearson, P.D. "The Effects of Grammatical Complexity on Children's Comprehension, Recall, and Conception of Certain Semantic Relations." In *Theoretical Models and Processes of Reading*. H. Singer & R. Ruddell (Eds.). Newark, Delaware: International Reading Association, 1975.

Peresich, M.L., J.D. Meadows & R. Sinatra. "Content Area Cognitive Mapping for Reading and Writing Proficiency." In *Journal of Reading*. Vol. 33, No. 6 (1990).

Piccolo, J. "Expository Text Structure: Teaching and Learning Strategies." In *The Reading Teacher*. Vol. 41, No. 9 (1987).

Pratt, M.L. *Toward a Speech Act Theory of Literary Discourse*. Bloomington, Indiana: Indiana University Press, 1977.

Readence, J.E., T. Bean & R.S. Baldwin. *Content Area Reading: An Integrated Approach*. Dubuque, Indiana: Kendall-Hunt, 1989.

Reid, J. "Learning to Think about Reading." In *Educational Research.* Vol. 9, No. 1 (1966).

Rosenblatt, L.M. *The Reader, the Text, the Poem.* Carbondale, Illinois: Southern Illinois University Press, 1978.

Rosenblatt, L.M. "Literature—SOS!" In *Language Arts.* Vol. 69, No. 6 (1991).

Ryan, E.B. "Identifying and Remediating Reading Failures in Reading Comprehension: Toward an Instructional Approach for Poor Comprehenders." In *Advances in Reading Research.* T.G. Waller & C.E. McKinnon (Eds.). New York: Academic Press, 1981.

Simpson, M.L. "The Status of Study Strategy Instruction: Implications for Classroom Teachers." In *Journal of Reading.* Vol. 28, No. 2 (1984).

Simpson, M.L. & S.L. Nist. "Textbook Annotation: An Effective and Efficient Study Strategy for College Students." In *Journal of Reading.* Vol. 34, No. 2 (1990).

Sinatra, R., J. Stahl-Gemake & N.W. Morgan. "Using Semantic Mapping after Reading to Organize and Write Original Discourse." In *Journal of Reading.* Vol. 30, No. 1 (1986).

Smith, F. *Comprehension and Learning.* New York: Holt, Rinehart & Winston, 1975.

Smith, F. & K. Feathers. "The Role of Reading in Content Classrooms: Assumption vs. Reality." In *Journal of Reading.* Vol. 27, No. 3 (1983).

Smith, R. J. & V.L. Dauer. "A Comprehension-Monitoring Strategy for Reading Content Area Reading." In *The Reading Teacher.* Vol. 28, No. 2 (1984).

Pugh Smith, S., R. Carey & J. Harste. "The Contexts of Reading." In *Secondary School Reading.* A. Berger & H.A. Robinson (Eds.). Urbana, Illinois: National Council of Teachers of English, 1990.

Spires, H.A. & P. D. Stone. "The Directed Notetaking Activity: A Self-Questioning Approach." In *Journal of Reading.* Vol. 33, No. 1 (1989).

Stahl, N.A., J. R. King & W.A. Henk. "Enhancing Students' Notetaking through Training and Evaluation." In *Journal of Reading*. Vol. 34, No. 8 (1991).

Stauffer, R.G. *Directing Reading Maturity as a Cognitive Process.* New York: Harper & Row, 1969.

Stauffer, R.G. *Directing the Reading-Thinking Process.* New York: Harper & Row, 1975.

Tierney, R. & P.D. Pearson. *Learning to Learn from a Text: A Framework for Improving Classroom Practice.* Reading Education Report No. 30. Urbana, Illinois: University of Illinois, Center for the Study of Reading, 1981.

Vaughan, J. & T. Estes. *Reading and Reasoning Beyond the Primary Grades.* Boston, Massachusetts: Allyn & Bacon, 1986.

Vygotsky, L. *Thought and Language.* Cambridge, Massachusetts: MIT Press, 1962.

Weinstein, C.E. & B.T. Rogers. "Comprehension Monitoring: The Neglected Learning Strategy." In *Journal of Developmental Education.* Vol. 9, No. 1 (1985).

Infotext References

Emmel, T. *Worlds within Worlds: An Introduction to Biology.* New York: Harcourt, Brace, Jovanovich, 1977.

Gross, H., D. Follett, R. Gabler, W. Burton & B. Ahlschwede. *Exploring Our World: The Americas.* Chicago, Illinois: Follett, 1982.

King, A., I. Dennis & F. Potter. *The United States and Other Americas.* New York: Macmillan, 1982.

Parker, C. (Ed.) *Textbook of Anatomy and Physiology.* St. Louis, Missouri: C.V. Mosby, 1967.

Silver Burdett. *Silver Burdett Science.* Norristown, New Jersey: Silvver Burdett, 1985.

Sund, R.B. et al. *Accent on Science.* Columbus, Ohio: Charles Merrill, 1982.